SHOCKING TRUE STORIES OF MURDER, CORRUPTION,
GREED AND COVER-UPS IN KENTUCKY

WHILE NO ONE'S WATCHING

DARLENE F. PRICE

Editing, design, distribution by Bublish

ISBN: 978-1-647049-75-1 (paperback)
ISBN: 978-1-647049-76-8 (hardcover)
ISBN: 978-1-647049-74-4 (eBook)
ISBN: 978-1-647049-77-5 (audiobook)

If men were angels, no government would be necessary.

—James Madison

The Expert Behind the Insights

Darlene Fitzgerald Price has over forty years of combined law enforcement and investigative experience: as a captain in the US Army Military Police Corps, serving with the Criminal Investigation Division; as a Special Agent in the Department of Treasury, US Customs Service; and as a private criminal defense investigator working with criminal defense attorneys on high-level drug and murder cases.

Beginning in 1979, Darlene competed for and won a full-ride Reserve Officers' Training Corps (ROTC) scholarship to Eastern Kentucky University, where she earned her bachelor of science degree in criminal justice/police administration, with a minor in military science. In this degree program, she completed many hours of extensive investigative training and proper processing of crime scenes. While earning her degree, Darlene also worked for a private security company, Andy Frain Security, in Lexington, Kentucky.

Upon Darlene's graduation from Eastern Kentucky University, she served on active duty and subsequently in the reserves as a captain in the US Army Military Police Corps. Darlene served in positions such as operations officer, where she was responsible for the management and supervision of an on-post police force including uniformed police and plain-clothed investigators. This included performing duties as a duty officer who was required to respond to crime scenes and supervise and assist the processing of felony crime scenes and proper collection of evidence. Some of the cases that Darlene was involved in are written about in her first book, *BorderGate: The Story the Government Doesn't Want You to Read.*

Darlene also served as executive officer for the office of Criminal Investigation Division (CID), and has testified as an expert witness in court martial proceedings and under the Uniform Code of Military Justice (UCMJ). Darlene's responsibilities have included, but were not limited to, the supervision and completion of interviews of witnesses and victims. Additional duties included training officer responsible for the organization, and supervision and hands-on training of the post police force. This included conducting training in the areas of investigation, crime scene processing, interviewing techniques, firearms training, surviving armed confrontation, proper arrest procedures, and constitutional law. While serving in the military, Darlene was awarded the US Army Commendation Medal for excellence in service.

After her time in the military, Darlene was hired as director of security for a large private security company called Recreational Centers Incorporated. Darlene was responsible for the day-to-day operations of a security police force and loss prevention investigators for several large resort condominium complexes.

Darlene was then hired as a Special Agent with the Department of Treasury, US Customs Service, assigned to the Office of the Resident Agent in Charge (RAIC) in Riverside, California, just east of Los Angeles. Darlene performed duties as a case agent for numerous large-scale narcotics smuggling and money laundering cases and operations all over southern California. Many of these were multi-agency, Organized Crime Drug Enforcement Task Force (OCDETF) cases targeting high-level Mexican and Colombian cartels. Darlene and her team successfully seized tons of narcotics and dozens of firearms. Darlene was required to conduct numerous interviews of witnesses and control confidential informants. Darlene and her team executed numerous high-risk search warrants, seized evidence, and processed crime scenes. Darlene also served as an undercover agent on significant cases with the Drug Enforcement Administration (DEA). Some of these cases are referred to in her first book. Darlene also conducted investigations into the importation of child pornography and served as a Department of Treasury, Secret Service, augmentee on personal protection details. Back then, there was no Department of Homeland Security. United States Customs Service, Bureau of Alcohol, Tobacco, and Firearms (BATF), Secret Service and Internal Revenue Service (IRS) were all under the Department of Treasury. Because of Darlene's prior military training, she and others were selected to perform duties with the Secret Service as augmentees on personal protection details with Bill and Hillary Clinton, Ronald Reagan, Bob Dole, the Israeli prime minister, and many other heads of state. While with customs as a Special Agent, Darlene testified as an expert witness in both state and federal court.

While serving with customs, Darlene received many hours of additional training including: extensive firearms training on numerous weapons including the Steyr AUG A3 M1 semi-automatic rifle; Driving While Under the Influence DWI law enforcement instructor training at Lackland Air Force Base, San Antonio, TX; certificate of graduation, criminal investigator training program at the Federal Law Enforcement Training Center (FLETC), Glynco, GA; US Customs Service Academy and Basic Enforcement School; Secret Service Protection Training, Burbank, CA; surviving armed confrontation, Office of Special Agent in Charge (SAC), US Customs Service, Los Angeles, CA; and numerous hours of specialized narcotics training from the DEA task forces with whom she served.

While serving with customs, Darlene received many awards and letters of commendation for outstanding performance including: serving with the Southern California Drug Task Force; commendation from the San Bernardino County District Attorney's Office for outstanding performance in the large prosecution of a narcotics smuggling organization; letter of commendation from Paul Clayton, Resident Agent in Charge (RAC), Santa Ana, CA, DEA, for distinguished work as an undercover agent on the Hector Casas operation; a letter of appreciation and cash award from the commissioner of customs for response and support of customs agents during the highly publicized Los Angeles riots; two silver medals and one bronze medal in the 1999 Police Olympics, Pasadena, CA, for swimming and cross-country events; and a plaque for outstanding performance with the High Intensity Drug Trafficking Area(HIDTA) Group 50.

Darlene left the US Customs Service her agency when she and others became whistleblowers on high-level corruption within the US Customs Service. During this time, Darlene gave live testimony on two occasions before the US Congress in support of tighter whistleblower protection laws for federal government employees on the front lines of our national security. She was honored with a plaque from the Government Accountability Project (GAP) and the Project on Government Oversight (POGO), recognizing her as a National Security Whistleblower. It was also during this time frame that Darlene was awarded a scholarship to attend law school from the Patrick Henry Center, awarded by founder Gary Aldrich (former FBI whistleblower and author) and former Congressman Bob Barr. Darlene then earned her Juris Doctor from Taft Law School.

After she left the federal government, Darlene continued to work as a private defense investigator on both civil and criminal cases. Three of these cases were high-profile murder cases, and one civil case that her husband, Austin Price, successfully argued before the Kentucky Supreme Court. During this same time frame, Darlene also worked as an investigative journalist for a local television and internet show entitled *Truth or Politics*. It was during these investigations that her and her team profiled numerous stories of waste, fraud, abuse of authority, cronyism, and corruption, exposing public officials and police agencies in the state of Kentucky. Some of these cases are profiled in this book, *While No One's Watching*.

Table of Contents

Introduction

Everything you are about to read is true. These events happened over the course of several years, from 2019 to 2024, and were derived from a series of reports by a small investigative news team in South Central Kentucky. This involved the thorough, time-consuming reporting of a TV and social media investigative show titled *Truth or Politics*. These events primarily occurred in a relatively small community in the middle of the Daniel Boone National Forest in Kentucky. Some names have been changed out of respect for the dead, the innocent, brave whistleblowers, confidential sources, and living victims. The names of the public officials and police officers that I am revealing have not been changed. I named this book *While No One's Watching* because this is what happens in governments anywhere when there is no oversight, no checks and balances, no audits, no inspections, and no transparency, and public officials are left to their own unchecked power.

We have a cancer of cronyism and corruption in the state of Kentucky, operating at will with virtually no oversight, within our small towns and in our state government. This cancer is indicative of the same type of disease that has infiltrated the top levels of our federal government, which I have witnessed firsthand. The investigative reports contained in this book are just the tip of a very dangerous iceberg that triggers grave concern. What you are about to read is a microcosm of a much larger problem in Kentucky and in our country. While it may seem as though I am picking on Pulaski County, Kentucky, it must be said that many other counties in Kentucky have very similar issues.

James Madison said, "If men were angels, no government would be necessary." I want to make it very clear that I am not anti–law enforcement, and I am *not* anti-government. I am very supportive of law enforcement and our system of government. However, I am very much against incompetence, cronyism, corruption, and a lack of accountability in law enforcement and our public officials. I still believe that here, in the good ol' US of America, we have the best system of justice of any place on earth. I still believe that most cops are honest and do a very difficult job to the best of their ability. I also believe that a small percentage of corrupt and incompetent public officials and cops somehow manage to finagle their way into management, usually through the good ol' boy system and "who's your daddy" backroom deals.

Most of the police officers in Pulaski County, the City of Somerset, and the Lake Cumberland area are good, hardworking cops who absolutely despise cronyism and corruption. Moreover, as I have now worked in Pulaski County and the Lake Cumberland area in Kentucky for several years now, I have gotten to know many of this area's good citizens. Most of the folks in this region are the salt of the earth. These are kind, generous people who are the type to give you the shirt right off their back. They are people who, when a funeral procession passes, pull over to the side of the road out of respect, even when they do not know the deceased. Most of them are the "I got your back" variety. They will avoid trouble as best they can and just want to live their lives in peace. However, don't piss them off or condescend to them. That will go over like a brick in the ocean.

The public officials that *Truth or Politics* and I have exposed on our news show and in this book are not representative of the good people of Pulaski County, McCreary County, and the Lake Cumberland area. These are the fine citizens that have, on many occasions, risked their jobs and retaliation by obtaining many of the documents and information that I needed to do my job. It is to these fine, brave souls that I dedicate this book.

How I ended a twenty-year career as a criminal investigator / Special Agent in the military and in the federal government, in Southern California and Fort Huachuca, Arizona, is a whole other story. I hope you will read about it in my previous book, *BorderGate: The Story the Government Doesn't Want You to Read*. It's safe to say things didn't end well in LA, as they rarely do. I became a national security whistleblower against my agency and gave live testimony before congress on two separate occasions. The details of the high-level corruption that I was blowing the whistle on are also detailed in my previous book.

After I left the US Customs Service (renamed by me as US Corruption Service) as a Special Agent, I went into private industry as a criminal defense investigator / case profiler, working for criminal defense attorneys. My husband was the county attorney and prosecutor in McCreary County, Kentucky, where we lived, making it a clear conflict of interest for me to work as a defense investigator in this County. I also worked in my husband's private law office as his investigator on non-criminal cases. Subsequently, I was hired by several defense attorneys in other counties in Kentucky, including Pulaski County, as an expert witness and/or private investigator.

In 2009, I was asked to host a small, local cable TV, internet, and radio show covering the news. I very quickly began using my investigative skills in this endeavor. I trained a small team to assist me, and we very quickly became a successful, investigative journalism show called *Truth or Politics*. This team consisted of a technology and mechanical genius; former/retired, well-trained, and experienced law enforcement personnel; exemplary attorneys; and former elite military personnel. At their request I am keeping them anonymous. However, this book and these investigations would not have been possible if not for their tremendous assistance. In addition to appearing on local cable television, we quickly went up on the internet, Facebook, and YouTube. Our forte was exposing waste, fraud, cronyism, corruption, and abuse of authority in public officials. Over the course of thirteen years, we were able to unseat or cause the outright firing of nineteen public officials. Each one of those nineteen stories of the exposed public officials could be an entirely different book. But for now, let's concentrate on the stories in this book.

Because of our success in McCreary County, I was being pleaded with to investigate issues that were happening in Pulaski County, which is located just north of McCreary County. For years I had heard rumors about just how corrupt some officials were in Pulaski County. These stories seemed too extreme to be true. However, as I learned from my days as a Special Agent with the US Customs Service, nothing would surprise me.

In 2018, the Harvard University's Center for Ethics released a study indicating that Kentucky had the most corrupt state government. It also detailed how Kentucky was second to none when it came to the legal corruption of political favors in exchange for campaign contributions. In 2019, the Institute for Corruption Studies (ICS) at Illinois State University listed Kentucky as one of the more corrupt states in the nation (you can view this study at https://greasethewheels.org). Ironically, in 2015, the FBI was referred to in an article by the *Louisville Courier Journal*, which stated, "Study after study continues to rank Kentucky as one of the most corrupt states in the country. It has been 23 years since the FBI completed the 'BOPTROT' investigation that resulted in the arrest and conviction of 15 members of the Kentucky General Assembly." Except for those fifteen convicted, I do not believe much has changed for Kentucky.

Chapter 1

CROSSING THE LINE

I never met a con artist I didn't like.

—Anonymous

It is important to understand that, for the most part, crossing the line for any public official or police officer usually doesn't happen overnight. Oftentimes it begins with bending the rules just a little bit. Then in increments, tiny steps over time, the rules are eroded. Officers and public officials are often way over the line before they even know it. Then they are trapped, and even if they wanted to find their way out, they don't know how. After that, it's about just self-preservation—sometimes at all costs. That's when people get hurt; that's when people get killed. The main ingredients for this are usually a combination of lack of training, lack of oversight, and a culture of impunity. These ingredients are a recipe for disaster.

When evaluating people in our society it is important to understand that 10percent of the American population falls under the categories of psychopath, sociopath, or narcissist. Unfortunately when normal people first meet someone new, they usually give them the benefit of the doubt.

The new person comes to them with a clean slate. When, in actuality, what normal people should be doing is beginning the evaluation of that new person with the question, "Is this person in front of me one of the ten percent?"

It is estimated that 1percent of the US population are psychopaths. It is estimated that 3percent of the US population follow under sociopath. Both of these personality disorders lack empathy for others. People with these disorders have a disconnect with societal rules of conduct or the rights of others, and they don't believe people are equal. They feel they have more rights than everyone else. Both feel their time is more valuable than your time and therefore have problems adjusting to changes they have no control over—changes not made by them.

The *Oxford English Dictionary* defines *psychopaths* "a person with a serious personality disorder that involves not caring about other people's feelings, not feeling sorry when they have done something bad, and wanting to be violent or cruel towards others." Psychopathy has been associated with DNA predispositions. Studies have shown that the amygdala part of the brain is thought to be dysfunctional. This area of the brain controls emotions. Psychopaths are unable to establish true emotional connections with others. They are emotionally detached from the behaviors they exhibit. They tend to form superficial bonds for their own personal benefit. Psychopaths never regret their actions, no matter the harm. Psychopaths usually commit crimes in a manner that poses the least risk to themselves. Children who exhibit callous unemotional traits, lack of empathy and guilt, and shallow emotions are more likely to grow up to be psychopaths. They tend to engage in aggressive and antisocial behavior, such as bullying. They will not develop lifelong friends since they cannot enjoy these bonds. Psychopaths are prevalent among serial killers. Some occupations that seem to draw psychopaths include CEO, police officer, attorney, and doctor. They are easily bored with mundane tasks or people. Psychopaths typically have a very strong and positive attitude and will give 100 percent effort on a project. They rarely exhibit dynamic ranges of emotions. Psychopaths tend to have a short attention span that mimic ADD or ADHD symptoms. Psychopaths frequently have abnormal thoughts because of the way their brains are wired. Pathological lying is a trait that many psychopaths exhibit. Lying is guiltless for psychopaths.

The *Oxford English Dictionary* defines *sociopath*s "a person who has a mental illness and who behaves in an aggressive or dangerous way toward other people." This is usually caused by a brain injury, childhood abuse or neglect, belief systems, and upbringing. They are usually a product of their environment. They have little conscience. They do, however, have the ability to feel remorse and guilt. Although they may feel empathy, they usually lack the ability to override their negative conduct. Unlike psychopaths, sociopaths have very dynamic ranges of emotions. They are highly impulsive. They have a difficult time keeping jobs. They prefer to work at the periphery of society. Like psychopaths, some occupations seem to draw sociopaths, for example, politician, doctor/surgeon, police officer, attorney, salesperson, CEO, professor, and clergyperson.

The Mayo Clinic describes narcissistic personality disorder as a condition in which people have an unreasonably high sense of their own importance. They often exaggerate their achievements. They expect favorable treatment. They may lack the ability to understand or care about the feelings of others. They lack empathy. They are usually arrogant, selfish, and often engage in bullying. They have a willingness to exploit others. Engaging in patronizing and condescending behavior is very normal. They are hypersensitive to criticism and react with anger. The careers that narcissists are most drawn to are politician, CEO, salesperson, police officer, and judge. The causes of this disorder are unknown. However, some studies indicate that genetic predisposition, early childhood trauma, child neglect, and parents who lack clear boundaries may contribute to these traits.

Despite what society tells us, our safety is ultimately *our* responsibility. It is incumbent upon us to become educated about these personality disorders and learn how not to be too trusting, especially with new people in our lives. Many con artists have one of the above listed behavior disorders. They have perfected a process for manipulating people. It's what they do. Who they target the most are people that have an inherent distrust of themselves, people who are insecure, and people who, in their nature, have to be dependent on someone else.

Some cops and public officials are simply and clinically narcissists and/or narcissistic sociopaths. Narcissists and sociopaths many times will overlap. These are some of the most dangerous folks in power. They enter public service with the covert intent of utilizing their positions to gain power and money. They use religion to disguise their real intent and become bullies to enforce their will on others. In the Bible Belt, it is easy for con artists to use religion as a prop. They take advantage of kind, religious folks who want to believe in their fellow man. This is a different breed from the honest cop or public official who becomes influenced and loses their way over time. These are con artists who, more often than not, con their way into powerful positions. In an environment with little to no oversight, these folks can get away with a great deal and exact a lot of damage before they are exposed.

But know this—the only way they can thrive and climb, as Edmund Burk was once believed to have said, "is for good men to do nothing." Unfortunately, under a bully's rule, good men fear losing their jobs, family, reputation, and sometimes even their lives. This is what a true narcissistic sociopath in power will go after in order to silence anyone who challenges them(a.k.a. whistleblowers). In many cases corruption is not something that happens somewhere else; corruption starts right here at home. Too often when people think of the word *corruption*, they think of DC or big cities. They are reluctant to believe this sort of thing can happen in their town or small community. They are reluctant to believe their neighbor who attends their church every Sunday could ever be a con artist.

Repeatedly in my experience, I found it quite disturbing just how easy it was for con artists and corrupt public officials to use religion and, predominately in this area, being a "Christian" as a prop to con people into believing they are good, honest people. If nothing else is learned from this book, I hope that citizens become much more discerning about the people they trust. Not everyone who attends church and sounds like a Christian actually is. I know that sounds cynical and I hate that I have to write it, but it is most necessary.

Con artists are very much predators and are oftentimes very clever chameleons who can take on any personality to fit their environment. Many times they are the very best brownnosers, which can make them the favorites of management. The cold, hard fact is that they are just wolves in sheep's clothing. Most people going about their lives, rarely see the signs until it's too late.

It is important for good citizens to know that simply giving blind trust, without verification, to anyone who portrays themselves as a "Christian" can be a dangerous thing. Narcissists, sociopaths, and even psychopaths (a.k.a. predators) are almost always multidimensional chameleons and very good con artists. They can easily hide in plain sight by using the blind trust of honest people who simply want to see good in others. My mom had a saying:"I never met a con artist I didn't like." I'm not sure where she heard this phrase, or if she coined it herself, but it always stuck with me.

As you read this book, I hope it helps you discern traits to protect yourself against con artists and disingenuous people. It is important to understand that these types of predators will always act and react for what is in their best interest. They are masters of deflection. If you catch them in the act of lying or some other type of dishonest behavior, they will never own it, so to speak. They will never take any responsibility or admit they were wrong or made a mistake. They will almost always react with condescension or by chastising the person who catches them. It's almost like they are saying, *How dare you question me or dare to point out my lies and deception.* They are never wrong, and either can't or won't apologize. It is always someone else's fault, or the person confronting them is overacting or needs to calm down and stop overreacting.

Once exposed there is always a massive disconnect between what others see and how they perceive themselves. There's an old saying, "It's easier to con someone than it is to convince them that they have been conned." I would also add "regardless of the evidence." I've come to believe the reason for this disbelief is that these victims become ashamed that they have been taken. They don't want people to think they were stupid enough to fall for this behavior. To these victims I want to say to you, there's nothing to be ashamed of. You did nothing wrong. Being a trusting soul is a virtue in today's world. You are not stupid just because you've been taken. Some of the smartest, well-educated people I know have been conned out of something. Everyone has been conned at some level in their lives, even me. The fault lies only with the con artist. You will be much better off if you place your focus on outing the wrongdoers, confronting them, and then forgiving yourself and moving on. Learn from this and educate others. Turn pain into purpose.

Unfortunately, over the past twenty years I have seen this disturbing culture of behavior within leadership in many of Kentucky's public officials, police departments, in their police academies, and in state and local agencies, like the Pulaski County Sheriff's Department. To fix a problem, you must first admit you have a problem. That is *not* what I see happening in Kentucky's law enforcement and in many government agencies.

I want to be clear that there are in fact many hardworking, dedicated cops in Kentucky. As I am writing this book, I am working with a state police detective in our county on an investigation that I have spent over eight years on. It involves school officials in McCreary County, Kentucky, and will be the topic of my next book. This Kentucky State Police (KSP) detective has worked harder than any cop I have ever worked with. On this case, he has worked after hours, weekends, and has run down every lead he has been given. He is as professional as it gets. I only wish more were like him.

However, with respect to law enforcement particularly, what I have witnessed as a result of numerous interviews and investigations is that these police training facilities and academies are very arrogant in what they teach. More importantly, there are no real good weeding out processes in these academies. The good ol' boy and good ol' girl attitudes are too prevalent in Kentucky law enforcement training facilities. Many of the academy instructors and leaders are retired KSP officers who are part of the good ol' boy system that got them the instructor positions, oftentimes without being the most qualified person. Unfortunately, in the state of Kentucky as a whole, connections matter more than competence. This becomes very incestuous and at the very least, creates conflicts of interest and resentment by officers who are excluded from and harmed by the cliques.

Further, the selection boards that are part of the process for selecting these academy instructors are mostly made up of the governor's handpicked political appointees. They are often not the best people for the job, but they helped the Kentucky governor or other state legislators get elected, and this position on a board is their reward. Most boards in Kentucky share this same profile and have a tremendous amount of power. The cream of the crop rarely gets to rise to the top, not only in Kentucky law enforcement but in other important government positions as well. This is not a partisan issue. Both political parties have shared in this problem over the years, and none have attempted to resolve it. This too is a recipe for disaster.

When you have this type of management selection in any law enforcement community, it lends itself to a cover your ass (CYA) culture, and Back the Blue becomes Circle the Wagons. I had a front row seat to this management style for years in my former federal agency and in some of the local law enforcement agency task forces I was assigned to.

One of the worst for this was the Los Angeles Police Department (LAPD). On one of the task forces I was assigned, we were using one of the LAPD's surveillance units entitled LA Effect (name changed). We were using them to wall off a wiretapping operation we had going involving a money laundering case and money stash house. The *Reader's Digest* version of this story is that several guys on this task force were skimming money on or before the takedowns. These were guys I would have never suspected in a million years of being dirty, yet they were.

How this worked was we would have cameras and a wire on a primary money stash house. When the crooks would go to move some of the money, we would follow them to the next location and then call out a separate local wall unit to set up surveillance on the secondary location. Oftentimes we would use LA Effect to take over surveillance and create separate probable cause (PC). This would build a wall away from the initial location where we had the wiretap and cameras set up so we could keep monitoring that activity without burning the wire on the primary money stash house. LA Effect would then create separate PC, enough to get a warrant or conduct a pretext stop as a vehicle was leaving the secondary location, thus building a wall between the primary and secondary location. What some of the officers on LA Effect were doing was, upon serving the warrant and/or pretext stop takedowns, they would take much of the money and it would never make it to the police station. The crooks weren't going to cry about some of their drug money missing because they were too busy trying to deny any association with it. These police officers knew this all too well.

The FBI caught on to this scam through a confidential informant and ended up arresting several of these officers. When the whole thing went down, I couldn't believe all who were involved. I was especially close to one of the guys because of the military police reserve unit we had both been assigned. This guy was a real family man and a stand-up kind of guy, or so I thought. This was my first gut-wrenching view of how someone good could go so very wrong. All of these guys did federal time, and on this rare occasion, the FBI actually did something about police corruption. I would later learn the hard way that this would be an isolated incident and not the common practice of the FBI. I would learn that the FBI will almost never go after other cops, especially if they were in another federal agency. This was a major part of my undoing with my former corrupt agency. To learn more about this, you may read my first book, *BorderGate: The Story the Government Doesn't Want You to Read*.

The same crony culture I saw within LAPD I now see in some of Kentucky's police departments and in the Kentucky State Police (KSP). This is a similar culture that begins with cronyism and lends itself to corruption. Unfortunately the genesis of this behavior is usually created by hiring boards and police academies where they are trained. In Kentucky, I have interviewed numerous sources, some of whom were instructors at Kentucky's police academies. I've even interviewed a couple who have resigned as instructors because of what they had observed as an atmosphere of cronyism.

In these interviews, on more than one occasion, I heard, "We just teach the basics here and expect that the officers will return to their departments and be further trained by their managers." One of the big problems with this line of thought is that there are no basic requirements to run for sheriff in Kentucky. In some instances, the sheriff is one of the least qualified people on the police force. They are elected officials and sometimes it is simply a popularity contest. That's not good! The Kentucky legislature could fix this by passing a statute that gives some advanced requirements to run for sheriff. I have spoken to several state legislatures about this, to no avail. Unfortunately, these legislatures have the same arrogance and refusal to recognize any problems not only in Kentucky law enforcement, but pretty much anywhere else in Kentucky government. They view anyone daring to point out real, documented issues as a troublemaker or someone who doesn't Back the Blue. In fact, look at the governmental stumbling in passing any meaningful legislation regarding special deputies and constables. Many in these positions have police powers but no law enforcement training or experience. Yet they are handed a badge and have the full power and authority to use deadly force. They are allowed to effect arrest and process crime scenes without attending any police academy and/or have little to no education, training, and experience. This has been nothing short of a disaster in Kentucky, and it could easily be remedied by our state legislature.

Further, over the past several years I've had the opportunity to interview numerous, diverse sources for this book. Some of them were expertly trained prior military, marines, and army infantry. These are people who have seen real combat operations in Afghanistan and in Iraq. They came back to Kentucky to become police officers. These folks were taught the importance of proper training and proper briefing of incursion operations, of breaching and clearing urban buildings and structures. Some of these young men were truly the real experts in this field in their police departments. Yet when it came time to execute something as important as a search warrant on a structure, someone much less qualified ran the operation. This all too often resulted in what the experts would call a Charlie Foxtrot (a.k.a. cluster fuck).Afterward, the real experts fully expected to have an after action report and briefing to determine what the weaknesses were and how to improve. This is what professional police departments routinely do and how I was trained in the military. However, when these soldier-cops dared to ask their police managers about this, they were scoffed at and put in their place by lesser-trained and lesser-qualified managers.

Good managers know their limitations and do not allow their egos to get in the way of expertise in the downward chain of command. A good manager recognizes this expertise and properly utilizes it. What I've seen too often, not only in Kentucky but in other states as well, is that police managers are afraid of looking weak by not being the smartest person in the room on every subject. Their egos cannot allow anyone else to shine other than themselves or their handpicked, often lesser-quali-fied cronies. This is even more prevalent when these managers face an election every four years and are in the public eye.

Another issue that is all too common in small communities is that cops and public officials are somehow related. Cops will tend to protect and defend their colleagues and family at all costs—even when common sense and clear evidence tells them otherwise. This leads to cronyism and a toxic police culture that forces officers to band together. This creates ethnocentrism, an "us against them" type of thinking, not only in police forces but in other public offices as well. This type of toxic culture breeds corruption and the covering up of corruption.

What Kentucky really needs is to have a state public corruption unit that answers to the Kentucky attorney general's office. It needs to be staffed by excellent, qualified outside agency investigators and people with zero conflicts of interest—not political appointees of the governor or the attorney general. This would operate similar to how the Office of Inspector General (OIG) used to operate, when it still had teeth. It would be charged with only investigations of public corruption in our state and local governments and police agencies, and have arrest powers. Currently the only agencies barely (and I do mean barely) investigating police and public corruption in Kentucky are the FBI and the KSP— and this has been done extremely poorly. Until we have objective, outside-trained professionals doing these types of corruption investigations, nothing will change. Things will simply get worse. Sometimes it takes someone from the outside with no conflicts of interest and an eye for objectivity to get things resolved. Until we have real objective oversight and transparency, not only in law enforcement but in other public offices as well, this state will continue to be labeled, and appropriately so, one of the most corrupt states in the nation. Our Kentucky legislature could cure much of this, if only they would open their eyes and do their jobs.

Chapter 2

STUPID IN KENTUCKY

Pulaski County, Kentucky, lies in t1he middle of the Daniel Boone National Forest, and its largest town is Somerset. One of its primary sources of income is Lake Cumberland. Lake Cumberland is a huge lake that flows into the Cumberland River, which flows downstream through Nashville, Tennessee. It is a very active tourism location for swimming, boating, fishing, hiking, camping, hunting, and water-skiing. It is also the primary source of drinking water for many of the people and wildlife in Kentucky and throughout Tennessee. This is a pristine, beautiful, heavily forested area that offers amazing wildlife: black bears, deer, elk, foxes, beavers, bobcats, mountain lions, squirrels, coyotes, wolves, coywolves, and bald eagles, to name a few.

To give you an idea of what I'm talking about, let's go back in time to a previous case in Pulaski County. I'm sure you've heard the phrase "crazy in Alabama" from the movie with the same name. Very soon you'll see why I named this chapter "Stupid in Kentucky." To fully understand the intensity of what you are about to read, I must take you back to April 2002—and, for the record, this falls under the category of "You can't make this shit up."

Sam Catron was a child when he witnessed his father, the Somerset city police chief, being shot in front of their home. Three thugs armed with a shotgun permanently injured Catron's father, who died seven years later when one of the shotgun pellets that had lodged near his heart shifted and killed him. This event would shape Sam Catron's life and was the clear motivation for him to later enter law enforcement. In 2002, Sam Catron was the Pulaski County sheriff, and running for his fifth term, when he was killed in a murder-for-hire scheme involving one of his former deputies. Catron was known for his crackdown on the local drug dealers in Pulaski County. Catron obtained his helicopter license so that he could conduct nap-of-the-earth (NOE) aerial searches for marijuana. He was one of the very few sheriffs in Kentucky who managed to get a helicopter for his relatively rural and small police force.

In April 2002, Sam Catron was attending a political rally at a rural fire station in Pulaski County. This was a typical fundraiser for fire departments in Kentucky, which included a fish fry, auction, and candidates for the various offices giving speeches. His opponent and former deputy, Jeff Morris, was also in attendance. Catron was only forty-eight years old when he was assassinated by a man named Danny Shelley. Shelley stationed himself on a hill across from the Shopville Volunteer Fire Department and shot Catron with a high-powered rifle as Catron was heading to his vehicle. Catron was carrying two cakes that he had bid on and won at the fundraiser to his police cruiser. He died instantly from a single shot to his head.

Now here's where the first set of *stupid* comes in. Shelley chose this location above all others, in a rural and heavily forested county, to execute his plan. The hill that Shelley chose was approximately seventy yards away and almost directly across from the fire station. This location had no real cover or concealment. Witnesses could actually see Shelley, wearing camouflage clothing with a rifle slung over his shoulder, fleeing the scene. This fire station was loaded with cops and firemen who were able to very quickly determine the point of origin of the shot. The shooter, with no real exit strategy, then tried to flee on a motorcycle to a highway where police could easily radio ahead and catch him. In law enforcement there's a saying, "You can't outrun a radio." Shelly lost control of the motorcycle and was quickly arrested not far from the crime scene by a Pulaski County sheriff's deputy, who was also a member of the Shopville Volunteer Fire Department.

There is no rule requiring criminals to be smart, so Shelley couldn't violate it. But he surely demonstrated a high degree of incompetence, even for a criminal. Anyone with half a brain would have picked a different location and used that motorcycle to flee on the many rural trails available in a forest where police vehicles would not have been able to travel. Not to mention shooting a beloved sheriff at a very public event with other cops who had radios and patrol cars to simply chase him down. As stupid as this already sounds, it gets worse.

The shooter, Danny Shelley, was working for Sheriff Catron's opponent for reelection, candidate Jeff Morris. Shelley, Morris, and a man named Kenneth White were coconspirators in this assassination. White had previously faced charges for possession of cocaine, and he wanted his buddy Morris to win the race so that Morris would allow White to continue his drug enterprise. An investigation revealed that White was also bankrolling Morris's campaign for sheriff. The shooter, Shelley, was an unemployed derelict with an arrest record of public drunkenness and assault. If Morris were to be elected, Shelley was promised a job as a deputy. With Catron out of the race, candidate Morris thought he could win. Morris had been a deputy for several years until he resigned the summer before Catron was murdered. Morris was working as a plumber at the time of his arrest for conspiracy to murder Catron. Catron was heavily favored to win the race and Morris became desperate. White helped orchestrate the plan to get Morris into the position of sheriff.

Now, when successful killers conspire to commit a murder for hire, they do so while using at least half a brain. No, not these guys. Shelley, when he fled the scene in front of the many witnesses (many of whom were cops), fled on a motorcycle owned by Morris—that's right, the man who was running against Sheriff Catron gave the shooter his motorcycle to use in the assassination. The purpose of a murder-for-hire scenario is supposedly to put distance between the triggerman and the person hiring the shooter. That's not what happened here. Candidate Morris gave the shooter his legally registered motorcycle as the escape vehicle. Further, when Shelley's cell phone was searched, it revealed that the last number dialed belonged to White.

After interrogation, Shelley rolled and implicated Morris and White. The next day, White was interviewed. During the interview, White offered to gather evidence against Morris, but the police declined. A search of White's house was conducted and Morris was present when they arrived at White's house. Police then drove White to the commonwealth's attorney's office for a second interview. During the search, White surrendered a microcassette on which he had recorded some of his phone conversations the previous evening. As the police drove him home, White told officers he had heard Shelley say the only way to beat Sheriff Catron in the election was "to blow his head off" and that Shelley had bragged about his own marksmanship.

The next day, Morris and White were arrested. Morris and Shelley entered plea bargains wherein they accepted sentences of life without the possibility of parole for twenty-five years in exchange for testifying against White. At trial, Shelley testified extensively about his relationship with both Morris and White. He also testified that he was afraid of White because he had bragged about killing people, always carried a gun, had once pointed his gun at someone's face during a business deal in Shelley's presence, and had warned Shelley never to cross him or he would hurt Shelley's family. He also claimed that several days before the fundraiser, Morris and White told him that Sheriff Catron intended to arrest, and possibly kill, the three of them before the election. He testified that White had financed Morris's campaign for sheriff and that the three of them had spoken several times about killing Sheriff Catron. He stated he had met White several years before, and they had been involved in the drug trade together.

Morris also testified about his relationship with White. Morris had previously been employed as a sheriff's deputy but had resigned because of a dispute with the sheriff over vacation time and allegations that he had stolen a wallet from evidence. Morris claimed that when he attempted to back out of the campaign financing arrangement, White threatened him and his family, claiming he had already committed two murders in another county. During their relationship, Morris learned that White was heavily involved in the drug trade. White eventually spent between $25,000 and $30,000 on the campaign (compared to approximately $5,000 of Morris's own money). He also testified that White originally claimed to want to help because Morris had helped save his brother's life. Morris claimed that White had approached him in the fall of 2001 and offered to help finance his campaign. A few months after his resignation, Morris decided to run against Sheriff Catron.

Both Morris and Shelley ultimately admitted they had pleaded guilty to avoid the death penalty. The men also testified that White held a grudge against the sheriff over a raid of White's house and the concurrent confiscation of a four-wheeler. Shelley further testified that he called White while waiting to shoot the sheriff, and White told him, "Don't let me down." They claimed that White suggested both the place from where Shelley was to shoot and the escape route he should take afterward. According to both men, Morris and White purchased the bullets for Shelley's rifle and White was present when they purchased a battery for the getaway motorcycle. Both Shelley and Morris testified that White participated extensively in planning and preparing the sheriff's murder.

Here again, there were no commonsense efforts of the coconspirators to distance themselves from the shooter. When you're plotting a murder and you want to distance yourself, you don't go to the store with the shooter and purchase rounds and then give him your motorcycle as the getaway vehicle. Needless to say, White was found guilty of complicity to murder. White was sentenced to life without the possibility of parole.

The long and the short of it is a beloved sheriff was gunned down in a conspiracy perpetrated by three idiots—a drug dealer, a wannabe, and a candidate. Kenneth White died in prison in 2018 of natural causes.

Ironically, triggerman Shelley's defense attorney was Mark Stanziano. Stanziano was a well-known, respected criminal defense attorney who in 2014 was gunned down outside of his office in Somerset, Pulaski County, Kentucky, in yet another senseless murder.

Again, this first story was just to give you a flavor of the underbelly of Pulaski County and not to besmirch a community that I have grown to admire in so many ways. I will now dive into my stories.

Chapter 3

LAKE CUMBERLAND: WHAT REALLY LIES BENEATH

It is important to note that this next story about Lake Cumberland takes place simultaneously with the stories of Mayor Keck, the Pulaski County sheriff's missing evidence, the Pulaski County murder case investigation, and the J.S. "Call me Daddy" Flynn case, all detailed in upcoming chapters. These stories have been separated here for cohesion, but you will notice the bleed-over between the different, but simultaneous, investigations. The Lake Cumberland case was the impetus for me looking into the Mayor Keck case, the murder investigation, and missing evidence case. Again, these cases happened during the same time frame.

As stated, because of the success of the *Truth or Politics* investigative news show in McCreary County, I was being implored by a number of people to investigate odd occurrences in Pulaski County, just north of us. There was a citizen's action group that was having meetings, and I was asked to attend. In February 2019, I finally relented and attended one of these meetings in Pulaski County. I must say, after the meeting it occurred to me that if one-tenth of the allegations that were being made concerning public officials and the cops were true, then "Houston, we have a problem." I did a quick dog and pony show for the group on what *Truth or Politics* was and how we operated. At the end of this meeting, I was approached by an elderly gentleman who had what I thought at the time was an amazing but unbelievable story. At first, I thought he was maybe a victim of dementia. His story just seemed that unbelievable. What he told me was basically that the mayor of Somerset had thwarted his contract. He claimed he had a contract to bring millions and millions of gallons of toxic waste in the form of leachate into Pulaski County for him to properly dispose of legally in his "leach fields." The mayor somehow "stole" his contract. Now you may be as confused as I was as to what *leachate* is and why millions of gallons were going to Kentucky. Keep reading, I'll explain.

I was just about to ignore this guy, because it sounded too crazy, when another younger gentleman approached me and told me that this was true. He explained that landfills have this run off liquid that is called leachate. Rainwater filters through the toxic waste placed in landfills. When this liquid comes into contact with buried waste, it leaches and draws out the toxic chemicals from that toxic waste. They explained that the Somerset wastewater treatment plant (WWTP) was accepting leachate from four different landfills, two of them in Tennessee.

They told me a time and place where I could verify their story. I could follow one of these tanker trucks full of this toxic waste from one of the landfills to Somerset, Kentucky. So some others and I did just that. The following week, we surveilled and filmed a tanker truck from a landfill in Kentucky to the Somerset WWTP. We filmed it going into the gates of the plant. I was astonished but not yet convinced that it was being disposed of unsafely or inappropriately.

The next day I hit the state of Kentucky EPA, the state of Kentucky water district, and the City of Somerset (Mayor Alan Keck's office) with what is called an Open Records Request (ORR). By law, any government entity has to turn over any official government documents that are not privileged in some manner when properly requested. The documents must be produced within a reasonable amount of time.

I immediately got stonewalled by the Somerset City Attorney John Adams. However, very quickly I received a mountain of documents from the state EPA and the state water district. Most of these documents were like reading a foreign language, so I contacted some experts for help. What two of these experts told me about these documents not only shocked me but seemed to shock them as well. One of them, from another state and who was heavily credentialed in this area, stated that they would have to "shut Pitman Creek down" due to the high levels of E. coli on numerous occasions. They also detailed that the numerous violations being given to the Somerset WWTP with zero enforcement were very concerning. It was clear from these state documents that there was a serious problem with this plant bringing in millions and millions of gallons of toxic waste and running it through a highly defective plant into a creek that empties out into Lake Cumberland, then to the Cumberland River, where millions of people, wildlife, and livestock get their drinking water. It was shockingly obvious that the consequences of this were a potential disaster.

At this point, perhaps you're thinking, *So what?* Well, here's the *so what* as I detailed in a letter with supporting documents to the Kentucky state EPA, the Kentucky Water District, the Kentucky attorney general and the federal EPA:

> Lake Cumberland in Pulaski County, Kentucky, is located in the beautiful Daniel Boone National Forest. It is a very active tourism location for swimming, boating, fishing, hiking, camping and water-skiing. It is also the primary source of drinking water for much of the people and wildlife in Kentucky and throughout Tennessee. Pitman Creek in Pulaski County, Kentucky flows directly into Lake Cumberland. Lake Cumberland then flows

into the Cumberland River, a primary water source that flows downstream to Nashville, Tennessee. Further, the outtake for the Pulaski County drinking water is a short distance (about a mile), downstream from where Pitman Creek flows into Lake Cumberland.

As a result of numerous records that I have received from the state EPA and the state water district via open records requests, I have serious concerns regarding the water contamination in Lake Cumberland and the Cumberland River.

My primary concern is that we have numerous documents that demonstrate that the City of Somerset has a defective wastewater treatment facility from at least 2016 through 2021. Despite this facility being repeatedly threatened by the State EPA, they have, for at least the last 2 years, added to this facility even more serious contaminates from landfill runoff called leachate. My investigation clearly demonstrates that this was done in order to secure at least $300,000.00 a year by the Somerset City Council. This information is of particular concern if the notice of **hexavalent chromium** came after the introduction of leachate to this treatment facility. My research demonstrates that leachate from landfills hold some of the most dangerous contaminates, including asbestos. Some of these landfills will have leachate that may contain "**Perfluorooctanoic acid**" also known as "**C8**" as well as C6 **hexavalent chromium.** Normal purification processes will not remove these types of contaminates which are known to be **highly carcinogenic and lethal to wildlife.** C8 does not break down and is referred to as, "Forever Chemicals."

The documents that I have received from the State Water District, the State EPA, the Regional Health Department and the City of Somerset tell a most gruesome story. These documents clearly demonstrate that Sinking Creek and Pitman Creek, which empty out into Lake Cumberland and then into the Cumberland River, have numerous, repeated serious "Out of Compliance Violations" for: E-Coli, Chronic Ceriodaphnia Dubia Pkv; CBOD; Suspended Solids, Total Ammonia Nitrogen (as N), and **MOST CONCERNING** is the June 8, 2018, letter referring to "**hexavalent chromium**" limits – also known as C-6. These many violations run at least from 2016 to March 2022. These violations were serious enough that the State Water Department repeatedly threatened that, "Violations of the above cited statutes(s) and/or regulation(s) are subject to a civil penalty per day per violation. Violations carry civil penalties of up to $25,000 per day per violation depending on the statutes/regulations violated." Yet, in the State EPA, the State Water District and Somerset's answers and/or documents provided, there were zero fines or penalties levied on either the City of Somerset or the wastewater treatment plant; even though numerous violations have been cited over at least a period of six (6) years.

At this point (2022), The City of Somerset Wastewater Treatment Plant alone has introduced at least 40 million gallons or more of Industrial Waste Leachate from four (4) different industrial waste landfills, not to mention the thousands of gallons of industrial waste from the local businesses that send their industrial waste to this defective plant. These businesses include medical facilities that are permitted for some of the worst contaminates imaginable, including C-6 & C-8. These landfills and businesses are permitted for "Industrial Waste" while the City of Somerset's wastewater treatment plant has only a general permit that is over twelve (12) years old.

Even more concerning is the reaction / cover-up from the Kentucky State Water District. Case in point, one of the documents in my possession is an e-mail between Diana Robertson, Pretreatment Coordinator for KY Division of Water, "**As a follow-up to an earlier conversation, there are currently no federal or state wastewater standards/limits for PFOA (C8), PFOS or PFAS. As a result, wastewater treatment plants in Kentucky are not routinely sampling for those parameters. I wouldn't expect to see sampling of industrial user discharges for those parameters either as there are no applicable limits.**" In other words, she is refusing to test not only Pitman Creek or Lake Cumberland for these deadly chemicals, but apparently the State of KY Water District hasn't been and is NOT going to test for these "forever chemicals"; even though, there is a very real chance that this facility, and who knows how many others, are introducing them to our precious water sources. You can't find what you are not looking for.

Moreover, there WERE standards/limits for PFOA (C8), PFOS or PFAS that were set by DuPont. DuPont paid out over $4 billion dollars in settlement agreements regarding this very thing in the state of Virginia. In these suits, the federal courts ruled that there were limits and that those limits were set by DuPont themselves; and that limit is 70 parts per trillion. That is the equivalent of 7 grains of sand in an Olympic-sized swimming pool. Anything more has been deemed UNSAFE! The fact that a high-level bureaucrat in the State Water Division has no knowledge of this I find incredible. Furthermore, what is even more incredible is in an interview with the Somerset Wastewater Treatment Director, she stated that she had no idea what was in the leachate from the landfills that is now running through this defective system and into Lake Cumberland.

Recently the Federal EPA listed the acceptable standards for C8 in drinking water as **ZERO!** In a recent press release (June 2022) the Federal EPA declared that, "There are no safe levels of PFAs (C8) in drinking water." They further clearly stated that these "Forever Chemicals" have been linked to a myriad of cancers.

Sincerely,
Darlene F. Price

So based upon an almost two-year investigation, hundreds of documents, and location filming and interviews, our show *Truth or Politics* published and aired a documentary entitled *Lake Cumberland: What Really Lies Beneath*. As of 2024, this film is currently posted on YouTube. It was also broadcasted on local cable television and on Facebook. It is important to note that during much of the time we were conducting interviews and filming on location, we were also in the middle of the COVID-19 shutdown. My film crew, the sources we were meeting with, and I were taking a great risk to go after this story. All of us, at one time or another, suffered through multiple bouts of COVID-19. This made the documentary even more difficult to complete, but the importance of our mission couldn't be understated.

There's an old saying, "the devil is in the details." When you are making extraordinary accusations, you must have extraordinary proof. Our investigation provided exactly that. Within this book is a small mountain of documents that contain thousands and thousands of details that prove each and every one of the accusations contained herein. I'm hoping not to get too bogged down in the minutiae of all the important details that make up this story. In the documentary, we actually publish well over 200 of the documents that expose, at the least, misfeasance by Somerset Mayor Alan Keck. It also shows the appearance of an attempted cover-up by City Attorney John Adams and a condoning blind eye turned to these events by the Kentucky State EPA and the Kentucky state water district. This documentary uses public records and statements to show a blatant disregard for public safety by the very people who were entrusted with it. Needless to say, this documentary absolutely throws these public officials under the bus in a very public way.

Before this documentary was finished, I tried to get a meeting with Mayor Keck, but I was stonewalled and sandbagged by City Attorney Adams. So my Pulaski County *Truth or Politics* guy, Stan Gleason (name changed), and I met with City Attorney Adams. It is important to note that this meeting took place almost a year before we released the documentary. I had asked for public documents in an ORR to City Attorney Adams months prior. My request included any and all documents regarding the bringing in of leachate from landfills. In Kentucky, these public officials are required to turn over any and all public documents requested under the Kentucky Revised Statutes. As the attorney general at the time had stated, "These are not a request, this is a law." Well, City Attorney Adams refused to turn over the documents without first having a meeting with us. In Kentucky no one is required to have a meeting with officials in order to obtain public documents. Consequently, the law required that City Attorney Adams produce these public documents. However, in an attempt to get the public records, we agreed to a meeting.

In this intense meeting, Adams tried to play stupid and acted like he didn't know what we had requested. The ORR clearly stated, "Any and all records regarding leachate." When he realized that we weren't falling for his act and going to back down, he amazingly had a few documents regarding—that's right, you guessed it—leachate. He stated several times,

"I'll have to research this and get back to you." Then, when I explained to him what I already had from the state water district and the state EPA, he began to sweat. He very quickly realized the cat was out of the bag. He still refused to produce the rest of the mountain of documents that I was confident existed, and he made several comments during this meeting, such as "This will destroy tourism in this county" and "This will bankrupt our county if this gets out." This he stated after assuring us he didn't know anything about leachate and would have to research it. My immediate thought was he had not expressed any concern or com-passion for the citizens whose health had been impacted by exposure to this inadequate treatment of leachate.

We eventually reported to the Kentucky attorney general's office the reluctance of City Attorney Adams to produce these documents. It only took a speedy eight months and, magically, the Kentucky attorney general's office forced City Attorney Adams to produce the documents—or at least most of them. I filed a complaint in the form of a letter lay-ing out this entire scenario to the attorney general's office. When the attorney general investigator emailed City Attorney Adams about the complaint, Adams stated, among other things, "I'm not really sure what she [Darlene]is requesting. She's wanting something about leachate?" Now keep in mind the ORR we sent to City Attorney Adams was very clear that we wanted any and all records surrounding leachate. We also reiterated this during our in-person meeting. Yet here he was in this email feigning ignorance to the attorney general's office—the ultimate display of unprofessionalism. I later published those emails in the Lake Cumberland documentary to show the extent to which City Attorney Adams had gone to thwart my attempts to obtain the documents.

Not long after our meeting with City Attorney Adams, Stan Gleason and I had a meeting with Diana West (name changed), the director of the Somerset WWTP, and one of the engineers. Both of them had signed off on and were referred to in numerous documents that I had already collected. The engineer just sat there like he was afraid and didn't say much during the entire meeting. His silence said more than any group of words could have expressed. West proved to be ever more illuminating. When I asked her if she knew what was in the leachate, she indicated she had no idea what was in it. I asked her if she knew what C8 was. She didn't know. When I explained to her what we had found and what we were doing, she began to cry. She stated, "This will ruin Somerset." I asked her who approved the contracts to bring this stuff in, but she would not answer. She just said, "I signed the contract, so I guess I'm responsible." Here again there were no real expressions of sympathy for the citizens who may have been exposed to these toxins.

Nevertheless, part of me felt sorry for her because she was obviously a patsy and a possible scapegoat for the higher-ups when something went wrong. She couldn't tell me much of anything that was going on with the leachate. She did produce some documents showing that millions of gallons of leachate had already gone through this defective treatment plant. I asked her if she knew about the numerous violations that the WWTP had been cited for by the state. She stated that, "The leachate money was how they were going to fix the plant." So that was apparently the thinking behind this brilliant idea: Let's bring in millions and millions of gallons of toxic waste from four different industrial waste landfills and run it through a defective treatment plant and then use the money to fix the broken down plant. What could possibly go wrong? Could you imagine the consequences of a truck driver using this type of logic to operate a defective truck? Would anyone be sympathetic to the argument that they were going to have the brakes repaired after they made enough money from driving it? No! People would be justifiably outraged if he harmed someone. Is anyone less outraged when the government does it? A government that is entrusted to protect the public.

I found it very disturbing that West really didn't know what C8 was and had no idea what was in this leachate. Anyone in this type of position should have been educated on both. She had no idea that this leachate came from landfills that accepted asbestos. But this is exactly the type of person you would want if you were trying to keep people in the dark: an unenlightened person who would sign contracts without asking questions.

Up to this point, I had never met then–Mayor Keck. Although I had met with City Attorney John Adams which, in military parlance, was a huge FUBAR (fucked up beyond all recognition) of a meeting. Keep in mind at this point, Mayor Keck was running in the primary for reelection, and our investigation into the Lake Cumberland leachate issue began two years prior to this election. As soon as the documentary came out, I was immediately notified by sources that Mayor Keck was saying that the documentary was just "political" because he was running for mayor. Again, I must reiterate, we began our investigation two years prior to the mayor's election, and it was none other than City Attorney Adams who caused an eight-month delay because of his dilatory production of the documents.

Later we were at a fundraiser for the Pulaski County Republican Party around a week following the debut of the documentary, and Mayor Keck stormed through over one hundred people, ignoring their questions (again, during a reelection) as he made his way across the room to our location. We were at the very end of the building, the opposite end of the entryway, set up with three cameras. One of my crew members said to me, "Get ready—here comes Mayor Keck."

He introduced himself. I responded with "I'm Darlene Price." Mayor Keck then said, "I know who you are; the sheriff pointed you out to me." With his demeanor and approach, I immediately took this as an intimidation tactic. If that was his intention, he failed.

There was a table next to us full of people listening to our conversation. I started firing questions at him that he tried not to answer, yet he couldn't help himself and kept talking. He kept asking why I didn't make an appointment with him to get his side of the story before we aired the documentary. I told him we tried to get a meeting with him but City Attorney Adams kept stonewalling us and insisted we only meet with him. I detailed to him how the ORR was sent to his office for a response, and the only person who responded was the city attorney who then played stupid and refused to turn over the documents. Mayor Keck then made a statement that I'll never forget: "Well he was just trying to protect me." He accused us and the documentary of just being "political" because he was running for mayor. I made it clear that I couldn't care less about this mayor's race and we would have gotten the documentary finished eight months prior if not for the stonewalling of his city attorney. The conversation lasted for several minutes and quickly deteriorated.

As he walked away, he left me with the impression that he was a con artist. Over my many years of education, training, and experience, I've had the luxury of interviewing numerous criminals and con artists. I knew after this short interaction that there was much more for me to find on this man. And boy, was I right.

That very evening, Stan Gleason received a call from the Pulaski County Sheriff's Department telling him that he was under investigation for a stolen car. That night Stan called me at about ten p.m. and explained what had happened. I instructed him to go to the sheriff's office on Monday and take a witness with him. I told him to take an ORR to the sheriff's office asking for any and all records for this investigation. I also told him to surreptitiously record his conversations with them on his cell phone.

On Monday, Stan called the sheriff's office and had a conversation with one of the supervisors. Stan recorded this interview, where he was in fact told that he was under investigation. He was told this was regarding a vehicle that someone had placed on one of his properties and left there, and Stan had allegedly had it towed off his property. In Kentucky, as in most states, if someone deposits or abandons a vehicle on your property, without your permission, you have a right to have it towed. So even if Stan did this, he would be within the law. Regardless, he did not have it towed. In fact, the night that he was accused of doing it, Stan was performing at a bar in front of about fifty witnesses. It seemed that this was an intimidation tactic by one of Pulaski County Sheriff Speck's deputies. Remember this name, Sheriff Speck, because you will read it many times in the following chapters.

The following day Stan went to the Pulaski County Sheriff's Office. Stan asked to speak with a supervisor. A supervisor, who we'll call Captain Roy, came to the desk to meet Stan. Stan very nicely asked him for information regarding the phone call he had received telling him he was under investigation. Captain Roy immediately became condescending and unprofessional with Stan and told him that he was not under investigation and that Stan was just trying to stir up trouble. Captain Roy's condescending demeanor only heightened Stan's concerns about the call. Stan then handed him an antecedently prepared ORR, to which Captain Roy continued to be condescending toward. Stan and his wife were secretly recording this event on two separate cell phones. Captain Roy stated that the caller (initial call on April 13) did not accuse Stan of stealing a car. Captain Roy further stated that someone had told the sheriff's department that Stan may have towed the car. He stated, "Nobody accused you [Stan] of stealing a vehicle. Dispatch put it in the system as vehicle stolen. Have your lawyer send us an open records request and I'll give you whatever you want." Stan made it clear to the officer that on this particular property, there are cameras available for anyone to view if, in fact, they were really investigating a supposed theft. Incidentally, the open record statutes in Kentucky do not mandate that a citizen hire an attorney merely to obtain public records.

On April 18, 2022, at approximately five p.m., Stan appeared in person at the Pulaski County Sheriff's Office with a completed ORR regarding this allegation. A deputy, "Dillon," took Mr. Gleason's ORR and gave him a stamped, dated copy.

On April 21, 2022, Mr. Gleason received, through the mail, a letter from Chief Deputy Major Jeff Hancock. This letter stated, among other things, "We do have an active investigation regarding the theft of a vehicle." This letter did not state whether Stan was in fact under investigation nor did it give any information regarding the vehicle.

On June 30, 2022, I personally faxed an ORR to the Pulaski County Sheriff's Office from *Truth or Politics*. In this ORR I requested the following:

> Please provide any and all records regarding any phone calls made from the Pulaski County Sheriff's office to Stan Gleason, (606) 271-4968, during the time frame from April 3, 2022, to current. This would include any data regarding the April 13th phone conversation (stated above), and the allegation regarding the vehicle referred to in the April 21, 2022, letter (attached). Please provide any and all records regarding any investigation on Stan Gleason. If there is no investigation, please provide any records indicating this. If for any reason you cannot or will not comply with this Open Records Request, please provide the KRS rules or regulations upon which you are relying. **TRUTH or POLITICS** is a news organization that broadcast on Cable T.V., YouTube, a Louisville Podcast and live on Face-Book. If you have any questions, feel free to contact me at the above listed numbers. Your cooperation in this matter is greatly appreciated.

Several days later I got a response to my ORR stating they could not provide any records because it was an active investigation. This was in direct contradiction to what Gleason was told when he went to the sheriff's department.

I immediately sent a complete report to the Kentucky attorney general's office regarding this incident and requested an investigation. About a week later, I got a call from a confidential source that an investigator from the attorney general's office was interviewing the sheriff and Captain Roy. About a week after this, Captain Roy retired from the Pulaski County Sheriff's Office.

Several months later we received a response to my and Stan's ORRs. This response had a letter and records from the Pulaski County Sheriff's Office. This packet included a police report that clearly indicated there was in fact an investigation into Stan Gleason on allegations of a stolen vehicle. The police report stated that the storage unit across from where this allegedly took place had cameras on it and that the officer would review these cameras. There was also a letter from the sheriff's office stating that the investigation into Stan Gleason was completed with no charges.

There is no doubt in my mind that the sheriff's office had intended to arrest Stan on this fraudulent charge. Had Stan not been in a crowd of people the night this allegedly occurred, and had there not been cameras on the location where this allegedly occurred, and had we not gotten the Kentucky attorney general's office involved, I fully believe Stan would have been arrested. I saw this as a shot across the bow and a clear intimidation tactic to silence *Truth or Politics*. As an investigative news organization, we had no choice but to fully investigate the peculiar events occurring in Pulaski County. Where there's smoke, there's fire, and there were red-hot cinders everywhere around Mayor Keck and the sheriff's office.

In May 2022, I attended my first Somerset City Council meeting. I was invited there by two city councilmen, John Ricky Minton and Jim Mitchell, who had watched the documentary on Lake Cumberland. They were genuinely concerned and had questions about leachate being brought into the defective Somerset wastewater treatment plant. These councilmen told me they didn't know anything about this until they watched the documentary. They hadn't seen the contracts and hadn't had a chance to even vote on this issue. I believed them to be honest men, and this turned out to be true.

As with most public meetings, citizens are allowed to speak. I got up and started asking questions of Mayor Keck and members of the council. Several of Keck's minions defended Keck's decision. There were three brave councilmen—John Ricky Minton, Jim Mitchell, and Jerry Wheeldon—who were genuinely concerned and dared to speak up at this meeting. Minton and Mitchell began firing questions at Mayor Keck. Mayor Keck engaged in a total disinformation campaign during this and all of these meetings, in what can only be described as an effort to totally mislead the public. He continually stated that the leachate was "fully treated and diluted" before it was placed into Pitman Creek.

The glaring problem with Mayor Keck's disingenuous assurances is that these forever chemicals (PFOs, PFOAs, C8) and asbestos cannot be treated or broken down by any wastewater treatment system, especially a defective one with numerous state violations. It was really simple: if E. coli was getting past this treatment plant into Pitman Creek at unsafe levels, then certainly anything else the same size or smaller was as well. This is not rocket science—it's just science. Moreover, the inventors of these forever chemicals, 3M and DuPont, spent over thirty years and billions of dollars trying to find a way to filter, clean, or somehow break-down these deadly forever chemicals, to no avail. Now I ask you, does anyone really believe that Mayor Keck has suddenly figured out what 3M and DuPont couldn't do with all of their resources?

At one of these meetings, in an effort to further mislead the public as to how safe his wastewater treatment plant was, Mayor Keck stated that he would gladly drink straight from the effluent, which refers to the wastewater after it has been allegedly treated and purified before being expelled into Pitman Creek, from this plant. Needless to say, Mayor Keck never drank from the effluent. In fact, meeting after meeting, we all took note that the mayor and city council members were drinking bottled water, not tap water. Convenience or safety concerns—you be the judge.

In October 2022, there was a letter from the Somerset plant supervisor to the Kentucky Division of Water regarding one of the many violations given to the plant for the spikes of E. coli in Pitman Creek. In this letter, the WWTP actually admits that the effluent pipes were full of "blood worm colonies." Now this is the same effluent that Mayor Keck told the public was so safe that he would drink it directly but didn't. Politicians saying things they obviously do not believe is not new. But when it directly affects your health and safety, it is disconcerting.

Prior to this council meeting, I had contacted the editor of the local newspaper, the *Commonwealth Journal*. His name is Jeff Neal. I had given him most of the evidence I had collected on this case, and he used it as the foundation for some enlightening articles. As you may imagine, Mayor Keck was furious. Neal did at least three front-page articles. On the last one he did an excellent job of laying out the danger of these forever chemicals. Neal was retired from the paper the following week. I suppose some people could not handle the truth. But hiding the truth doesn't kill it; it only conceals it. Even though the local paper was buckling under political pressure, I knew this story was too important to the health of our community to ignore it.

Whoever said, "You can't fight city hall" was wrong. Several city council meetings later, participation had swollen to over fifty citizens in attendance. It was standing room only. A local attorney also got involved in this fight to stop toxic waste from coming in. The now-educated citizens were demanding this be stopped. In this meeting, I fired off questions to City Attorney Adams. Adams actually admitted he had not read any of the contracts involving this leachate. One of the concerned city councilmen asked him, "Why didn't you read them? Isn't that your job?" Adams responded, "I don't always read the contracts." Many of us found this statement to be incredible, and we surmised that it was his way of ameliorating his role in bringing in this dangerous and toxic waste. Another reason to question City Attorney Adams regarding his lack of review of the leachate contract was because we had directed his attention to this very thing months earlier in our meeting and in an

ORR. This prior meeting and ORR were in direct contradiction to what Adams was selling at this city council meeting.

In this same meeting, Mayor Keck admitted that only a city employee had signed this multimillion-dollar contract—he never did. When the councilmen stated that they didn't know anything about the leachate and they didn't get to vote on it, Mayor Keck responded, "You knew. It was in the budget that you voted on." The brave councilmen John Ricky Minton and Jim Mitchell argued vehemently against Mayor Keck in a scathing debate.

It became clear from this interaction that Mayor Keck had cleverly buried the leachate contract information within numerous lines of a very extensive, over $90 million city budget. The council members were never fully advised as to what leachate was, never knew that the Somerset wastewater treatment plant had received numerous violations from the Kentucky State Division of Water, and never had a chance to discuss and vote on this important issue. This appeared to be yet another good ol' boy /"who's your daddy" backroom deal to anyone following this story. Unlike many of these deals that only involve fleecing taxpayers, this one risked the health and safety of our community and countless others downstream. As such, this issue should have been decided in a stand-alone meeting with public input.

About a year prior to this council meeting, Stan Gleason and I sat across from City Attorney Adams and told him precisely what documents we wanted, one of which was any contract involving this leachate. This was also included in our ORR to the city that Adams had responded to by demanding a meeting before he would turn over any documents. It is doubtful that any attorney in his right mind would choose to not research this issue and read the contracts in light of this previous meeting. This is especially true given our meeting with him, the submission of our ORR, and following the Kentucky attorney general's office getting involved. Adams either read it and misled the city council or chose the path of plausible deniability by continuing to play stupid. Or he engaged in a level of incompetence so extreme that it is rarely seen by human eyes.

At one of the last meetings involving leachate, there was again standing room only from concerned citizens wanting this to be stopped. Keck kept trying to end the meeting and walk out. The concerned councilmen and crowd wouldn't let him. Things got loud and people were angry. One of Mayor Keck's minion councilmen, Robin Daughetee, repeatedly echoed Keck's drivel about how safe the water was. Incidentally, this councilman had also repeatedly spoken to me in a condescending manner. A citizen of the audience began to challenge Councilman Daughetee. This citizen was a well-built man who looked like he could handle himself well. Councilman Daughetee talked down to this gentleman, much like he had previously spoken to me. The citizen got red-faced and began to roll up his sleeves and step toward Councilman Daughetee. He told Daughetee, "You're not going to talk to me like that!" I truly thought Daughetee was about to get his attitude checked. It was obvious that Councilman Daughetee also thought the same thing. Councilman Daughetee, being the typical bully bureaucrat he was, immediately changed his tone and apologized to the man. It is amazing how accommodating a disrespectful bureaucrat can become when they are faced with the consequences of their actions.

Also at this meeting was a kind gentleman who stood up and told the story of his wife's cancer. He spoke about how she had never smoked, ate right, and exercised her whole life. He also stated, "The one thing my wife did every day was drink lots of water from the spigot in our home." The man began to cry as he told what he and his wife were going through. He told of how the type of brain cancer she had was the type that scientists and the EPA had linked to these forever chemicals. When he was done, there was not a dry eye in the room. His story was pivotal to what would happen at the end of this meeting.

Another lovely lady told her husband's story of how he had gotten cancer and their subsequent struggles. She told of how the doctors all told them his cancer was caused by an environmental issue when they lived in Ashland, Kentucky. Then she stated that was why they had moved to Somerset, to get away from impurities in their water. She stated that had they known this was happening, they would have never moved to Somerset.

After several more citizens mustered up the courage to stand and share their concerns, I leaned over to Stan Gleason and said, "It's like I told you, courage is contagious." Keck kept trying over and over again to end the meeting and silence everyone. He kept saying, "Citizens comments are over" and tried to stand up and walk off. The good-guy councilmen wouldn't let him. At the end of this heated, emotional meeting, the council finally voted unanimously to stop the leachate. Keck was furious and glared at me with an "if looks could kill, I'd be dead" expression. I just smiled back because I had not done this to make him happy but rather to prevent people from getting sick.

We left the building, walking to the parking lot outside. There was a group of folks, including the two brave councilmen, who motioned me over. One of them said to me, "Do you have some kind of security?" To which I answered, "I pack heat everywhere I go." He then stated, "Good, because you're in danger. You just caused some very powerful people a whole lot of money and you need to be careful." Stan Gleason then said, "I told her that. This is what we [at *Truth or Politics*] do." I then added, "Yeah, this ain't our first rodeo. Keck and his cronies can just stand in line." The next day my husband installed a GPS tracker on my vehicle. He stated, "When you disappear, at least we'll know where to start looking." I felt bad because I knew he was worried about me. I told him, "Sorry, you knew what I was when you married me." We both laughed because he has stood up to his share of bullies too.

At a council meeting about a month later, a local attorney stood up and told the council that he had his drinking water tested, and there was in fact small amounts of forever chemicals detected. One of the problems is that these chemicals, even in the smallest amounts, are deadly.

The trucking contractor who was bringing in the leachate had a sunset clause in this contract for ninety days. By the time the leachate was stopped, we estimated that well over sixty-five million gallons of leachate was processed through this highly defective wastewater treatment plant, with full knowledge of the state EPA and the Kentucky Energy and Environment Cabinet (a.k.a. the state water district), all of which turned a blind eye. This toxic waste would most certainly flow downstream into the Cumberland River, all the way to Nashville, Tennessee, and beyond.

In September 2022, the Kentucky Energy and Environment Cabinet released a study that found that forever chemicals were contaminating Kentucky fish. The report stated that the chemicals had already been found throughout the Ohio River, in every major Kentucky watershed, and at unsafe levels in at least thirty-eight drinking water systems. They cautioned to not eat the fish in these areas.

On August 26, 2022, the federal EPA proposed new laws concerning forever chemicals that basically lowered the allowable amount of these chemicals in our drinking water to virtually zero.

In March 2023, the federal EPA held a national press conference on the dangers of forever chemicals. The director was quoted as saying the following:

> The EPA proposed limiting the amount of harmful forever chemicals in drinking water to the lowest level that tests can detect, a long-awaited protection the agency said will save thousands of lives and prevent serious illnesses, including cancer.
>
> The plan marks the first time the EPA has proposed regulating a toxic group of compounds that are widespread, dangerous and expensive to remove from water. PFAS, or per- and polyfluorinated substances, don't degrade in the environment and are linked to a broad range of health issues, including low birth weight babies and

kidney cancer. The agency says drinking water is a significant source of PFAS exposure for people.

In March 2023, I was asked by the federal EPA to give live testimony, via Zoom, in support of the proposed EPA bill before Congress. I was only given the standard five minutes, but I talk fast. I was able to condense the story about Mayor Keck and referred people to our documentary. This would be the third time I would give testimony before our US Congress.

In June 2023, the Centers for Disease Control and Prevention (CDC) released a study saying the state of Kentucky has the highest cancer rate in the nation. In what would be the ultimate irony of this story, the state of Kentucky filed a multibillion dollar lawsuit against DuPont for its release of forever chemicals in April 2023. In that suit, landfills were specifically mentioned as a source of the forever chemicals contaminating our lakes, rivers, and streams here in Kentucky. When I read this, I couldn't believe the hypocrisy of our state, turning a blind eye to landfill leachate and defective treatment plants, then having the gall to file suit against DuPont. Not that I'm justifying what DuPont has been accused of. Indeed, DuPont has proven itself to be a bad actor and certainly should be made to pay for its transgressions. However, this does not relieve the state of Kentucky from its sanctimonious dealing with equivalent polluters. After this lawsuit was filed, I obtained a copy and read directly from it at the very next Somerset city council meeting. Mayor Keck simply glared at me as I fired questions at him regarding the similarities of the allegations in the lawsuit and what they had been doing. For the most part, he and his minions just sat there, simultaneously looking angry and foolish.

While Mayor Keck and his minions are not solely to blame for this statewide fiasco, the Kentucky Energy and Environment Cabinet certainly are complicit in turning a blind eye to what Mayor Keck and his minions were allowed to do for years. We may never know just how many are like Mayor Keck in Kentucky, and are doing similar things and getting away with it. I found it absurd that the Kentucky Energy and Environment Cabinet filed suit against DuPont for introducing forever chemicals in our waterways but ignored what Mayor Keck and his minions did. DuPont's attorneys will have a field day with the hypocrisy of our leadership in Frankfort on this issue.

Again, this happens while no one is watching.

Chapter 4

MAYOR KECK INVESTIGATION

About halfway into our fight to stop the millions of gallons of toxic waste from coming into Pulaski County, I began an investigation into Mayor Alan Keck. He had been reelected mayor of Somerset and quite frankly, he just really pissed me off. The very first time I spoke in front of the city council, he called me a liar and did everything he could to completely mislead the public on the truth about the leachate and his defective wastewater treatment plant. Just weeks after he was reelected mayor, he threw his hat in the ring for governor of Kentucky.

The University of Somerset (a.k.a. the Bridge to Nowhere)

In his first term, Mayor Keck made a grand declaration about how he was going to bring a private, nonprofit research foundation to the City of Somerset, calling it the University of Somerset. After receiving numerous critical reports, I began securing documents concerning the mayor's supposed private Christian college. First, I learned that the University of Somerset and the University of Somerset Research Foundation weren't approved by the IRS as a charitable organization until November

2019. In an interview with Mayor Keck in 2019 during the COVID-19 pandemic by students of Somerset Community College, a real and established college in Somerset, Mayor Keck clearly stated that this will be a private university funded by donations, and the intent was that no taxpayer money would be used. He further stated in this interview that he had about $6million in pledges. As of December 2024, this interview was still on YouTube.

One of the documents I obtained was the deed to the property where this supposed college was to be built. To my surprise the deed to this property showed that the City of Somerset (a.k.a. Somerset taxpayers) had purchased this property in June 2020 for a cool $1million. The deed also had Mayor Alan L. Keck's signature on the deed (yeah, boy, no conflict of interest here). The City of Somerset then paid for the clearing of this property (formerly called Cundiff Square), a land survey for another $6,500, and a report of preliminary geotechnical exploration for $4,800. This was all approved by Mayor Keck for his "private" university to be paid for by taxpayers. The Somerset taxpayers also doled out over $6,200 to Interstate Environmental Services Inc. for a "survey/inspection for asbestos contaminating building materials" for the address of 200 South Vine Street, Somerset, Kentucky (a.k.a. Cundiff Square / the University of Somerset). Additionally, the taxpayers were also hit with an $8,300 bill from Integrity Architecture PLLC for a feasibility study for Cundiff Square. Again, all with the approval and signature of Mayor Keck.

Mayor Keck had listed on his tax records and with the Kentucky Secretary of State that he was the chair and director of the University of Somerset. We later learned that the dean of this establishment was none other than Keck's brother, Michael Keck. The foundation's 2019 tax return (Form 990) stated that the foundation received $750,800 in contributions. These contributions were a far cry from the $6 million pledges he boasted about in his earlier interview. Most of this was from one single contributor. Also on the 2019 tax return Form 990 was a claimed expense of $182,136. Of this, $173,720 was listed as "contract labor." It is unclear what this contract labor included. Part IV, page 2, line 1 of Schedule L on the Form 990listed "Michael Keck" as "family" receiving $25,000 for "non-employee comp."

The foundation's next tax return listed $44,225 in contributions. For expenses, Mayor Keck's brother, Michael Keck, received $10,417 as reportable compensation. Also listed was $106,246 for "contract labor." Again, it is unclear what this contract labor included. The problem with the $173,720 "contract labor" and the $106,246 for "contract labor" for these two years is that the City of Somerset (a.k.a. taxpayers) actually paid for that property to be cleared and researched, not the foundation.

As incredible as it sounds, the tax filings show that the foundation spent $268,532 to raise only $44,225 in its second year. Again, this was a far cry from the $6 million pledges he boasted about in his earlier interview. The question is: Was Mayor Keck exaggerating in his prior interview in order to make this Somerset university sound more feasible than it was, or did the contributions disappear after donors learned of Mayor Keck's incompetence in managing the leachate disposal?

Mayor Keck has publicly stated that no director ever received any compensation for this university. However, as with other matters involving Mayor Keck, the records show otherwise. Director Michael Hall received $100,000as compensation under part D, reportable compensation from the organization. Further, in Section A, item number 2, the following question is posed: "Did any officer, director, trustee, or key employee have a family relationship or a business relationship with any other officer, director, trustee, or key employee?" Keck clearly placed an X under the "No" box. This is diametrically opposed to the fact that his brother clearly played a role in this university and received at least $25,000.It is unclear on the tax returns who received the $173,720 for "contract labor."

Truth or Politics dedicated a show on the "Bridge to Nowhere" university, and I posted on social media the tax returns, deed, invoices, and the like for all to see. Needless to say, neither the University of Somerset nor the University of Somerset Research Foundation was ever built, and the taxpayers of Somerset absorbed well over a million dollars in costs for this bridge to nowhere. Ironically, Somerset University ended up providing taxpayers with an expensive education anyway. Again, this happens while no one is watching.

Living It Up on the Taxpayer's Dime

In late 2021, I received confidential source information that Mayor Keck was running up some costly credit card bills on a card paid for by the City of Somerset (a.k.a. taxpayers). I sent the City of Somerset and Mayor Keck a new ORR. Once again, I was sandbagged by City Attorney John Adams. It took over eight months before I got the records, mostly from confidential insiders, and what they revealed was astonishing.

Bear in mind this was in the months leading up to the 2023 Kentucky governor's primary election that Mayor Keck was campaigning for heavily, as candidates have to. In statewide elections in Kentucky, candidates have to successfully campaign in the heavily populated cities of Lexington, Louisville, Frankfort, and northern Kentucky. If you do not secure votes in these areas, you are out. Perhaps it is only a coincidence that is where much of Mayor Keck's spending took place, in mostly resort hotels and high-end restaurants. In about a two-year time frame, he spent well over $30,000 of taxpayer money via the city credit card. He also made numerous trips to Nevada, Alabama, Georgia, Florida, and Tennessee—just to name a few.

Mayor Keck spent $838.97 at a Marriott in Key West, Florida. He spent $1,974.01 at a Marriott resort in Tampa, Florida. He spent $249.09 on a suite in Naples, Florida. He spent $711.66 at the lavish Renaissance Birmingham Ross Bird Golf Resort and Spa in Alabama. He spent $6,615 in Lexington, Kentucky, at resorts; $4,883.87 in Louisville, Kentucky, at hotels; $1,300 at a convention center in Virginia; and $1,250 at the Dana Inn Marina in San Diego, California—hundreds of dollars on goodies and coffees for his staff and literally thousands of dollars on marketing companies to teach him and his staff how to manage and market. It is important to note that during this time frame, Keck was touting at city council meetings about how they were going to have a shortfall in the budget and would have to eliminate emergency responder positions (fire and emergency medical services). Many feared that Mayor Keck was using this ploy to bring back the leachate and the money it made.

When I received Mayor Keck's spending information, *Truth or Politics* posted the receipts, and I did a thorough investigative report on this. I was shocked at the response. More citizens were furious about his lavish vacations on their taxpayer dime than they were about him bringing in millions of gallons of toxic waste into their county. I kid you not. People were commenting on how they work their rear ends off but could never afford a Key West resort vacation or a trip to Vegas. This story fired them up much more than the Lake Cumberland leachate story. I think it was the resentment they felt at having to do without in order to pay taxes just to have a politician self-indulge using their money.

Kentucky has rules about using taxpayer money to campaign for a different office, or so I thought. I turned these documents over to the Kentucky State Board of Elections. As of November 2024, I am unaware of anything being done.

In May 2024, I was the defense investigator in a Pulaski County murder trial with attorney Jim Cox. Mayor Keck was in the jury pool. Before voir dire, Judge Whitaker called Mayor Keck to the bench. She asked him if he could be an impartial juror with me on the defense team. Mayor Keck feigned disbelief at having his impartiality questioned. He stated that he didn't know why I didn't like him but that he has nothing against me. This was just another example of Mayor Keck's poor acting skills. Judges have good poker faces, but I imagine Judge Whitaker mentally rolled her eyes as she smiled and dismissed him from the jury pool.

On September 26, 2024, the Kentucky League of Cities executive board appointed Mayor Alan Keck to serve on its board of directors. This, despite the fact that all you have read was exposed for everyone to see. Again, you just can't make this stuff up.

Chapter 5

MISSING EVIDENCE

An article by Jacob Ryan posted in News Break Magazine on January 14, 2025, stated, "a Kentucky Center for Investigative Reporting review of state records shows 25% of law enforcement agencies failed to submit reports detailing what they took last fiscal year through a process known as asset forfeiture, a powerful and controversial practice that police praise and civil liberty advocates denounce."

Again, I want to reiterate that many of the cops in the Pulaski County Sheriff's Department and the Somerset Police Department are good, honest cops who hate what is going on in their departments. Some of them have risked their jobs and safety to get me some of the information you are about to read in the next several chapters. These are the real heroes of this story. Further, while it may seem that I am picking on Pulaski County, it must be said that the issues in this county mirror what is happening in other counties in Kentucky. After numerous interviews of defense attorneys, police officers and defendants in other counties, I am convinced that as bad as Pulaski County is, it is not the worst. Not to beat a dead horse, but many of these issues can be solved at the legislative level by passing simple laws and regulations that most states have already passed years ago. But again, before you can fix a problem, you must first admit that you have a problem, and that's not happening within Kentucky leadership in Frankfort.

The events of the next several chapters were taking place almost simultaneously as I was exposing the leachate of Lake Cumberland and the Mayor Keck stories. As citizens observed me at city council meetings and on my show *Truth or Politics* standing up against the mayor and his minions, they began funneling me incredible amounts of information that seemed almost unbelievable. As I have stated many times, "courage is contagious." For weeks I had been getting information that there was a relatively large amount of currency and evidence missing from the Pulaski County sheriff's evidence room. Such an intriguing story was too important to ignore, so *Truth or Politics* began our investigation.

Remember, this story came to light during a pandemic. My team and I were literally meeting informants in dark alleys and locations far away from Pulaski County in order to retrieve much of this information and many documents. One thing I noticed about these informants was that they were seriously concerned for their life and the safety of their families if anyone ever discovered their identities. Their fear of the clique of very powerful people who run this county was palpable. They perceived these people as a bunch of bullies who would do anything to stay in power and not be exposed. This was very similar to what the good cops in my former agency (US Customs, now known as US Immigration and Customs Enforcement, or ICE for short) were going through as we exposed high-level corruption. As Yogi Berra is quoted as saying, "It's like déjà vu all over again." If my *BorderGate* story taught me anything, it is that the safest place to be is in the light and there is nothing I hate worse than cronyism, cliques, and bullies. These three things are precisely what breed corruption. I have been fortunate enough to have a brilliant husband who has backed my play at every angle. As a prosecutor and an honest attorney, he hates cronyism, corruption, cliques, and bullies as much as I do. I could not have exposed these stories without his help.

Over the course of several years, I had numerous people tell me that I was in great danger for exposing these stories. On one occasion, I was working for a local defense attorney as an investigator. I was waiting in the hall for him to finish some hearings. As court ended, one by one people came out of the courtroom. I had no less than three people, two of them criminal defense attorneys, say to me, "You're alive!" They were astonished that I was still alive after what I had exposed. To say that I would become public enemy number one to certain officials in Pulaski County would be an accurate statement. I, once again, began to remote-start my vehicle—a technique I learned after becoming a national security whistleblower after exposing high level corruption in US Customs years ago.

The timeline of these stories matters because of the bleed-over to the upcoming chapters, which involve a botched murder investigation by the Pulaski County Sheriff's Office and the removal of the Pulaski County court clerk by the Kentucky Supreme Court. I'm going to tell these stories separately, but know this—the missing evidence and currency detailed herein had not only an effect on a particular murder case but also several other criminal cases that would be upcoming. I received the following memos in January 2022. These memos, in and of themselves, tell a very interesting story.

When currency went missing from the sheriff's office evidence room, it was reported to the KSP. Kentucky State Police Detective Michael Keeton was assigned to investigate. The missing evidence story actually began in 2015.Detective Keeton's official investigative report (detailed below) establishes that, "The first case with missing currency was opened on August 04, 2015." Prior to this, on March 17, 2015, Detective Daryl Kegley, from Pulaski County Sheriff's Office, sent a typed memo to Sheriff Greg Speck, referenced "Evidence." This is a verbatim quote from the memo:

> On January 5th, 2015 I was given the task of conducting an inventory of the evidence room at the Pulaski County Sheriff's Office. As of January 1st, 2015, the evidence room has been on "lock down" status and every entry into that facility has been logged and witnessed by a second deputy. No items have entered into evidence storage since that time, and all items submitted for evidence have remained in the temporary lockers. That process has come to a completion and the results of that inventory will be submitted along with this memo. During the process, a few items listed in the inventory system were said to be in the evidence room, that at present time are unaccounted for.
>
> With that information in mind, these items that are unaccounted for could not have been present when you took control of the Pulaski County Sheriff's Office. The unaccounted items may be presently at the Kentucky State Police crime labs being analyzed. When these items return we will update the inventory book to reflect their return.
>
> Attached on page 2 is the list of items that are presently unaccounted for. I am requesting once if you feel

this inventory is satisfactory that you will sign off and allow us to reopen the evidence room for intake of new items.

The memo was signed at the bottom by Detective Daryl Kegley. Accompanying this memo was the list of items missing from evidence. This list contained the criminal case numbers for each item and names of suspects and victims. I have deleted the names of victims and case numbers for obvious reasons. Here is the list:

- Pulled head hairs "suspect name," Destruction Order

- Swab of Blood from cedar chest, Destruction Order

- Tennis Shoe with Blood

- Item 40,Photos of Victim "victim's name"

- Clothing Victim Wore Home

- Buccal Swab

- 1 iPhone A10000286B6AA5

- Bulova Watch Box

- Oakley Sunglass Box

- HP Laptop Charger

- Bushnell Trail Camera

- Five 20-Gauge Rounds

- Item 1

On August 13, 2015, another memo was generated and initialed by Major Jeff Hancock regarding change of evidence custodians. Here's the exact wording of the memo:

> Effective August 13, 2015, Administrative Sergeant Glen Bland, Unit 1116 will be assigned as the Primary Evidence Custodian for the Pulaski County Sheriff's Office. Detective Bobby Jones, Unit 1110, will no longer be the Primary Evidence Custodian, but will be assigned as Secondary Evidence Custodian.

This memo is particularly interesting because Detective Bobby Jones, who was removed as primary evidence custodian after missing evidence was discovered, later became the Pulaski County sheriff. He is also heavily involved in the upcoming botched murder investigation that I detail in upcoming chapters.

On October 19, 2020, Investigator Cody Cundiff was listed as the secondary evidence custodian.

On November 9, 2020, Deputy Jonathan Williams (a.k.a. Jon) was rehired as primary evidence custodian by Sheriff Speck. In KSP Detective Keeton's report he documented the following:

> Williams stated when he returned as the primary evidence custodian in November of 2020 he decided to organize and make use of the limited space the office had for the storage of evidence. Williams stated the evidence room was a mess. Williams stated he discovered numerous final judgments requiring evidence be disposed of. Williams stated he started on one side of the room and completed an audit of the general evidence. Williams stated he and Captain Troy McLin conducted an audit of the currency seized. Williams stated they quickly noticed the money missing from evidence.

Williams stated after Sheriff Speck learned of the missing funds he requested additional audits. Williams stated him and Cody Cundiff, who was serving as the secondary evidence custodian conducted another audit of the entire evidence room. Williams recalled he was cleaning out the evidence office desk due to the lack of a filing system and discovered an empty evidence bag among the final judgment paperwork. Williams confirmed the evidence bag was one of the cases with missing currency.

Williams said he informed the sheriff of the discovery. Williams said Sheriff Speck asked him to treat it as evidence. Williams described how he discovered a second evidence bag with money inside of it, in the same drawer. Williams stated he collected the two bags as evidence.

In November 2020, Williams clearly stated that he notified Sheriff Speck of the missing currency; however, Sheriff Speck waited until February 10, 2021, to report this to the KSP for investigation. Sheriff Speck should have known that not just money was missing, but he only reported the money. It is important to note that Sheriff Speck had previously retired from the KSP as a commander before running for sheriff.

Further documented by Detective Michael Keeton in his report was that on December 17, 2020, the evidence door lock was replaced. This was over a month after the discovery of the missing currency. Anyone who has ever been responsible for an evidence room knows, and common sense would dictate, that this lock should have been changed *immediately*, not weeks later.

On February 8, 2021, a memorandum from John Williams to Major Hancock was written regarding an evidence audit. Here is a pertinent excerpt from the memo, verbatim:

> I have conducted a complete audit of the evidence room and have discovered several items which are shown to be in the inventory yet they are unaccounted for. Items which are missing include cash, electronics, narcotics and other miscellaneous evidence. A list of the missing evidence is attached to this memo.

> Signed John Williams, Evidence Custodian.

This list contained three pages of evidence with case numbers and thousands of dollars of missing currency involving nineteen separate cases. Some of these items included several computers, iPads, laptops, Amazon Kindles, computer games, USB storage devices, GPSes, Smith & Wesson 9mm handguns, wallets, cell phones, drugs, surveillance discs, tools, designer clothing, coins, jewelry, keys, and numerous pieces of DNA evidence.

This list was in addition to the list of missing evidence found in 2015 and included an even greater number of items. Ironically, since they found missing items in 2015, not only was the problem not solved, it actually became worse. It was clear that many of these items were ones that could be easily sold for cash. However, the most disturbing aspect of this breach was the theft of DNA evidence. Once DNA evidence is tampered with, or in this case removed entirely, it becomes useless in future criminal prosecutions. The person, or people, doing this had become even more emboldened over time. They obviously felt very comfortable that they would either not get caught or nothing would happen if they did. This had the potential to allow criminal defendants to go unpunished or perhaps wrongly convicted. It would also deny crime victims of any sense of justice. This was a serious matter to the people involved in the cases that this evidence had been collected.

On February 10, 2021, Sheriff Greg Speck sent a letter to the KSP Commissioner Phillip Burnett. It is important to reiterate that Sheriff Speck was a retired, high-ranking supervisor with the KSP. The exact wording in the memo was as follows:

> Commissioner Burnett:
>
> A full inventory of the Pulaski County Sheriff's Office evidence room was recently conducted. The inventory revealed a sum of United States currency missing from the evidence room. I submit this letter formally requesting the Kentucky State Police conduct an investigation into this matter. Thank you in advance for your assistance.
>
> Signed Greg Speck, Pulaski County Sheriff.

I found it concerning when Sheriff Speck only reported the missing money ($25,697) and made no mention of the pages and pages of other missing evidence. Yet in the KSP police report dated February 10, 2021—completed by Detective Michael Keeton, under the heading INCIDENT DATE/TIME OF 8/1/2015 TO 2/10/202—as the time frame of the theft. Now, why would you put a date in 2015 if you had no knowledge of the 2015 memos and missing evidence? In a hearing in September 2022, almost two years after this investigation was opened, KSP Detective Keeton testified that the only missing evidence he knew of was the currency. This hearing is covered later in the book, in chronological order as this case takes place. But just remember this report—the devil is in the details.

KSP Detective Keeton was assigned to the missing currency case in February 2021. He would eventually complete his investigation in September 2022 after a hearing about this missing currency and other evidence before two skilled criminal defense attorneys and a savvy judge.

It is not clear why it took so very long to complete this investigation. Could it be because Detective Keeton was investigating a sheriff who was a former KSP commander, and he was slow-walking an investigation until the sheriff could retire? Or could it be that the snail's pace of the investigation was because there was an ongoing election for the office of Pulaski County sheriff that involved a former KSP officer?

After its completion, I pretty quickly received a copy of Detective Keeton's report from a reliable, confidential source. I would eventually obtain a redacted version of this through an ORR from the KSP. The contents of this report are disturbing. What was even more disturbing was the information that was omitted. The investigation was not thorough, and interviews that should have been completed were not. This report, although lacking in a comprehensive investigation, was about 200 pages long. I detail the most important aspects of this report in chronological order, as I try to analyze why these things were not completed.

On February 10, 2021, Detective Keeton was contacted about this case, as was stated in his report. Again, at this point there is no mention of other missing evidence, only money. One of the first paragraphs of his report documents the following: "1225 HRS- Detective Keeton spoke to Sheriff Greg Speck by phone. Sheriff Speck stated in October of 2020 the Primary Evidence Custodian Deputy Glen Bland resigned suddenly. Sheriff Speck stated he rehired retired Deputy John Williams to be the primary evidence custodian for the department in November of 2020. During a complete evidence audit, it was discovered that currency was missing from the evidence room. Sheriff Speck stated the Sheriff's Office has two accounts for currency seized as evidence. They have a seizure account and a forfeiture account. During the audit, they discovered seized currency had not been deposited into either account. Sheriff Speck stated they have since removed the remaining seized currency held as evidence to the seizure account awaiting court orders before transferring the funds to the forfeiture account." Again, no mention here of any other missing evidence, only missing currency.

On February 24, 2021, Detective Keeton reported that he had conducted three separate interviews of Lieutenant Daryl Kegley, Deputy John Williams, and Investigator Cody Cundiff regarding their assignment as primary and secondary evidence custodians of the Pulaski County Sheriff's Office's evidence room. All three denied any involvement in the theft of funds from the evidence room. A summary of the completed interviews was attached to the case file. What is missing from this investigation and report is the fact that Detective Bobby Jones was not interviewed as a suspect, even though he was clearly the primary evidence custodian at one point and then later removed from that position. During part of the time frame of this investigation, Deputy Jones was running for sheriff of Pulaski County.

On February 24, 2021, Detective Keeton documented the following in his report:

> During the initial contact with Sheriff Greg Speck and the interview with Deputy John Williams I learned additional information about the two evidence bags recovered from a desk drawer in the evidence room office desk on January 19, 2020. Deputy Williams had completed an internal report (121-0 1-0024) detailing the discovery and collection of the two bags. According to Deputy Williams while looking through the bottom desk drawer in the office at unfiled property reports and final judgments he discovered the two bags. Deputy Williams internal report reflected he found evidence bag (Item #2) first that was empty and appeared cut along the bottom opposite of the seal. After discussing the discovery of bag #2 with Sheriff Speck, he collected and photographed it as evidence. He further discovered evidence bag (Item #1) in the same stack that also appeared cut, however the

bag had $147.00 in cash inside of it. I have attached a copy of the internal report to the case file.

This is important because these two evidence bags with more missing money was discovered in January 2020, yet Sheriff Speck only reported missing currency to the KSP in February 2021. Now I know time flies, but why was this only reported to the KSP by Deputy Williams, not Sheriff Speck, and why over a year later? This alone should have caused Detective Keeton to treat Sheriff Speck and Detective Bobby Jones as suspects, just as much as the others, and they should have remained suspects until they were cleared. They should have been interrogated and polygraphed. As I will detail, Speck and Jones were never properly interviewed, interrogated, or polygraphed like the others. The unanswered question is why? Did politics play a role in this?

Security in the evidence room at the Pulaski County Sheriff's Office seemed to function more as a suggestion than as a necessity. The evidence system in place at the time was electronic. When deputies seized evidence, they had to return to the evidence processing office at the sheriff's office to complete the evidence process. They were supposed to log into the evidence system and complete the information for each item of evidence. A label was then printed and attached to the evidence bag or evidence item prior to placing it in a temporary wall locker, which opened from the back, within the secured evidence room. It was later discovered that a major problem with this method was that anyone could log into this system and access any case, not just the officer's specific case. At this point they could then change the evidence being presented to the locker. This created a vulnerable process that was ripe for exploitation. No evidence room should have a system that is this faulty.

In Detective Keeton's February 2021 report, he stated, "There is approximately seventeen cases dating back to August 04, 2015 to November 21, 2018 with missing currency. The approximate dollar amount missing is $25,697.00. One case file (N 15-08-0 148) is completely missing from the Pulaski County Sheriff Office." That is right. Not only were there pages of missing evidence and currency, but there was reportedly an open case file completely missing from the sheriff's office.

On February 24, 2021, Detective Keeton documented the following from his interview with Deputy John Williams: "Williams again reviewed the evidence system and discussed the fact some property other than money was missing, and that he was in process of tracking everything down. Williams' goal was to rule out if the missing property had been disposed of or returned to the owner. Williams advised he had started keeping an electronic copy of the property release form in addition to a hard copy in a file cabinet which sits in the sergeant's office. Williams and Detective Keeton reviewed the hard copy files and noted none of the funds missing were reflected in any of the property release forms."

Here again, Deputy Williams told Detective Keeton about nonmonetary evidence missing, not just currency. Yet in September 2022, over a year later, Detective Keeton stood in front of Circuit Judge Whitaker, under oath, and said no when asked, "Was there any other evidence missing other than the money?" Once again, I can only deduce that either Detective Keeton never really looked at the evidence being presented to him in this missing evidence case, paid no attention to what the officers were actually telling him in those interviews, or he intentionally misled Judge Whitaker while under oath. Any of these obvious conclusions are a display of a highly deficient investigation. And again, the question is why? Was it laziness, incompetence, or just good ol' fashioned politics?

Further detailed in Detective Keeton's report with Deputy Williams on February 24, 2021, was the following: "Williams stated if the currency were sealed in an evidence bag with a label affixed, there would be no reason for the evidence custodian to open the sealed bag. Williams stated he did not think that once the evidence label was printed, an evidence custodian could change it within the system. Detective Keeton and Williams reviewed the evidence system program again and determined an evidence custodian could in fact change the currency amount."

This faulty system could be exploited at will by miscreants. Anyone with access to the evidence computer could change not only the currency amount but anything they wanted to change regarding any type of evidence. No one would be the wiser since the evidence room was not properly audited or inspected. In fact, under this system not even the officer securing the items into the evidence room had to be notified.

On February 24, 2021, Detective Keeton documented that "Detective Keeton met with Major Jeff Hancock at the Pulaski County Sheriff's Office. Items of concerns in regards to the missing case reports and items needed moving forth. Major Hancock stated he would be doing the internal affairs investigation."

The actual report regarding this internal affairs investigation by Major Hancock would only surface after Judge Whitaker ordered the Pulaski County Sheriff's Office to turn it over before the Faubush-Norfleet murder trial, which was to begin in April 2024. I had submitted several ORRs to the sheriff's office and, each time they denied my requests, claiming it was still under investigation. After reviewing the so-called internal affairs investigation just before the murder trial in 2024, I was convinced there was no real investigation by Major Hancock into the missing evidence and currency. In one of his interviews of the wife of the main suspect, Investigator Cody Cundiff, Hancock spent more time chatting about his physical ailments and me, Darlene Price, than he did any viable questioning of this potentially valuable witness. In my expert opinion, this was not a serious internal affairs investigation. A short book could be written on the lack of investigation and inept investigative techniques employed by Major Hancock during this internal affairs investigation.

Again, this happens while no one is watching.

On February 24, 2021, Detective Keeton interviewed Pulaski County Sheriff's Office bookkeeper, Terry Brum (name changed). Among other things, the interview included the following: "Brum discussed how she documented the transaction records in early 2015 due to the lack of records kept by the evidence custodians. She recalled how they would bring her money with an amount written on a notepad. Brum was adamant she had to have a record of the transaction and photocopied what information she had available to document the transaction on her end. Brum was certain the money missing from the evidence room was not given to her. She stated she had searched for the case numbers, amounts, and names associated with each case." The interview further details that". . . years ago the receipt process was very generic. Brum stated the department did not have a seizure account in the beginning and utilized only a forfeiture account. She discussed how seized money was stored in the closet of the old evidence room upstairs. At that time, she was only given money from the evidence room when the funds were forfeited, and an order was obtained. Brum believed they started the seizure account in 2010 based on the QuickBooks Register Report printed June 22, 2021."

In other words, there was very little accountability and a computer system that anyone could alter at will with no accountability. This was a godsend to assist any dishonest officer in making currency and other evidence disappear.

On February 24, 2021, Detective Keeton conducted an interview with Lieutenant Daryl Kegley of the Pulaski County Sheriff's Office. Among other things, Keeton documented: "Kegley served as the primary evidence custodian until March of 2015. The evidence room for the sheriff's office was upstairs and was moved in May of 2016. Kegley discussed issues with the evidence room back in 2014 and 2015. He stated things were just not filed properly. Kegley stated a full audit was completed in January of 2015 when the current sheriff took office."

Once again documenting that in January 2015, Sheriff Speck knew he had problems with this evidence room and appeared to do basically nothing. Kegley also confirmed again that Deputy Bobby Jones was the primary evidence custodian in 2015. Yet Detective Keeton would barely interview Deputy Jones and did not polygraph him at all. The question again is why?

Also in the February 24, 2021 interview with Kegley was the following: "Toward the end of the interview, Kegley mentioned Bland had told him he had done a full audit. Kegley said when he done a full audit it resulted in a large three ring binder, which he currently cannot find. Kegley questioned if Bland had completed a full audit then he should have a record. Kegley stated he would try to find his audit binder for review." And now we have a large three-ring binder missing. It is unclear if this binder was ever located.

On March 3, 2021, Major Hancock provided a USB drive containing video footage from the evidence room to Detective Keeton. Major Hancock stated that, "the video was not of best quality and only went back approximately sixty days. The video has two camera shots labeled GV [gun vault] and ER [evidence room]. The video provided reflected recordings from December 1, 2020 through February 26, 2021. The two angles provided reflect Deputy Williams primarily doing his daily task. Others were also observed in the evidence room with Deputy Williams present. Viewing the video and knowing if a theft was taking place would be difficult based on the circumstances and unknown incident dates."

In any evidence room, there should be a storage of videos going back years, not just sixty days. This is especially true given the capacity of storage devices and the importance of evidence. With modern information storage devices (SanDisk memory cards, hard drives, and thumb drives), one can easily store several months of video in an evidence room very cheaply. And what is the point if you cannot tell what date and time you are later watching on the video camera or even observe the most important angles of that evidence room? Again, the sheriff's office management should have identified this problem years ago and made the appropriate corrections. This was not done.

On March 9, 2021, Detective Keeton scheduled three polygraphs for March 24 and 25 for Lieutenant Daryl Kegley, Deputy John Williams, and Investigator Cody Cundiff. Remember, on October 19, 2020, Investigator Cundiff was listed as the secondary evidence custodian, and in 2015, Detective Bobby Jones was the primary evidence custodian and was removed from that position. Yet Jones was not scheduled for a polygraph and neither was Sheriff Speck. Obviously if you know you are a suspect in this type of case and you are told you are about to face an interrogation from a state police detective, you would become preoccupied with that thought. Any cop facing this type of scrutiny in any agency should never be assigned to be the lead investigator in a murder case—but that is not what happened here. Again, timelines are important and the devil is in the details.

On March 18, 2021, Investigator Cody Cundiff was dispatched to be the primary investigator for a murder case on Faubush-Norfleet Road in Pulaski County, Kentucky. This was in spite of Investigator Cundiff being notified that he was, in fact, a suspect in the missing evidence/currency case and would be facing an interrogation and polygraph just days later. Bobby Jones would be dispatched to this murder scene as well, not knowing what the outcome would be of the missing evidence/currency investigation. In military parlance, this would prove to be a FUBAR in the making, which I will carefully detail in the next chapter. As you read previously, these cases are partially united and actually happen simultaneously. Please keep this in mind.

On March 25, 2021, Investigator Cody Cundiff, who is now the lead investigator in a murder case that took place just one week prior, on March 18, was polygraphed on the missing evidence/currency case. In KSP Detective Keeton's report, he detailed the following:

> Upon completion of the polygraph, Investigator Cundiff was interviewed briefly by Examiner Webb and Detective Keeton separately after the report was reviewed. Investigator Cundiff was asked by Examiner Webb how he did on the exam to which Investigator Cundiff

replied "fair." Examiner Webb informed Investigator Cundiff he did not pass the exam. When questioned by Webb, Investigator Cundiff denied taking the money. Investigator Cundiff alleged he never took the money and alleged he did not go in the evidence room often. As the questioning by Examiner Webb continued Investigator Cundiff further denied taking the money. Examiner Webb ended the interview at that time.

Detective Keeton informed Investigator Cundiff he had concerns with him currently and feels like he is involved to some degree. Investigator Cundiff denied being involved. Detective Keeton informed Investigator Cundiff he could leave and he would be contacted for further questions later. Detective Keeton notified Sheriff Speck of the results and expressed his concerns regarding Investigator Cundiff. Detective Keeton was later notified by Major Hancock that Investigator Cundiff was removed from his role in the evidence room this date. A copy of the three Polygraph Reports are attached to the case file. The reports reflected that Deputy Jon Williams and Lt. Daryle Kegley polygraph exams did not indicate any deception. The report for SGT. Cody Cundiff reflected that deception was indicated.

Further documented in this interview with Investigator Cundiff was that "Detective Keeton explained to Investigator Cundiff the currency amount could be changed after the seizing deputy printed the label. Investigator Cundiff alleged he did not know that was possible."

Any department leader should have known that a cop under this type of long black cloud should not be investigating a murder case. In any other department, Investigator Cundiff would not have been assigned to a murder investigation. There are many other avenues Sheriff Speck could have taken, but that is not what happened here. And again, the question is why? Why didn't Sheriff Speck take control of this murder case and assign it to someone else? If he had no one else qualified, why didn't he come to the crime scene himself and handle things? I guess the old saying "the buck stops here" just didn't apply to the Pulaski County Sheriff's Department.

It wasn't until June 22, 2021 that Detective Keeton got around to interviewing (not interrogating, not polygraphing) Lieutenant Bobby Jones. Of all the sheriff's office employees who had direct access to this evidence room, Jones had the shortest interview despite him being primary evidence custodian in 2015 and being removed from that position, then subsequently being secondary evidence custodian for many years.

On April 14, 2022, KSP Detective Keeton received the Automated Fingerprint Identification System (AFIS)report regarding the two recovered evidence bags. The report indicated that "no latent prints of value were recovered for comparison."

On June 28, 2022, Kentucky Association of Counties (a.k.a. taxpayers' insurer) issued a check for the reimbursement to Sheriff Keck for $25,447 minus a $250deductible.

It wasn't until July 2022 that Detective Keeton obtained search warrants for the account users who had access to the records for the fifteen court case files linked to the cases with missing funds. Nothing like waiting over a year to get a search warrant. In any investigation, time is of the essence. Detective Keeton must have confused the first forty-eight hours with the first year. This investigator waited over a year to simply apply for and receive warrants that should have been done before Investigator Cundiff was ever polygraphed. The information obtained from the warrants should have been used for questioning by the polygrapher during his interviews of Investigator Cundiff. At the very least, these warrants should have been conducted immediately after Investigator Cundiff failed that polygraph. Again, it begs the question why? Was this investigation slow-walked in order to not mess with the sheriff's election or perhaps to protect one of KSP's own?

As incredible as it sounds, on August 17, 2022, Detective Keeton received a call from Sheriff Speck in reference to a missing master evidence key to the evidence room. This report documents that "the missing master evidence key was found in the trunk of a PCSO pool vehicle (#1134). Sheriff Speck stated the key was secured and did in fact work on the old evidence lock removed in February of 2021."Apparently a deputy discovered the master key while cleaning out a trunk of a Pulaski County Sheriff's Office vehicle. The vehicle was utilized as a motor pool vehicle and driven for transports and other department needs. The keys to the motor pool vehicles are stored in a key box in the front office of the Pulaski County Sheriff's Office. The motor pool vehicle keys are accessible by any employee with access to the sheriff's office.

Now, if I'm a nefarious deputy or employee who wanted to cover up that I was the one who had been taking the evidence and money from that evidence room, this would be a good way to muddy the waters and widen the suspect pool. It would make it appear as if anyone could have had access to the evidence room via the master key. This should have never happened. Master keys to anything involving something as important as evidence should have been tightly controlled and well-documented with a physical sign in and out log. This too was not done, and the result has been nothing less than disastrous.

Documented in an interview by Detective Keeton on August 17, 2022, was the following:

> Detective Keeton also met with Randy Goff who was hired by the PCSO as the new evidence custodian. Goff had collected the evidence key and placed it in evidence. Goff also provided the old evidence lock that was kept in the evidence room after being replaced. Deputy Williams had secured the lock in the evidence room after it was

replaced. Deputy Goff confirmed he had checked the discovered key did work the Kaba brand evidence lock removed on February 19, 2021. The lock was originally replaced on January 14, 2021 with a new lock that was later determined to be faulty. The old lock was used again until the arrival of the new lock (Memorandum dated February 26, 2021).It was explained to Major Hancock and Deputy Goff the master evidence key located gave access to the room, once inside the evidence room access to the key box on the wall would allow access to the gun vault door, and wall locker. Major Hancock was not aware the master keys to the other doors or wall locker were stored in the key box.

In other words, the key box held the master key and other keys that could be used to access the gun vault room and the wall locker cabinets where the currency was stored. Keep in mind this is the same Major Hancock who conducted the incredibly poor internal affairs investigation into this evidence room.

On August 17, 2022, Detective Keeton further documented the following in his report:

Major Hancock was asked about Investigator Cundiff's access to the master key when Bland resigned. Major Hancock agreed it was possible Cundiff could have had access to the evidence key when he was assigned as the secondary custodian. Major Hancock recalled that Sheriff Speck had taken the evidence card (access card) from Cundiff when he was removed as the evidence custodian, after the polygraph. Major Hancock stated Sheriff Speck had given him the evidence card, which was locked up in a file cabinet. Major Hancock was certain he had provided it to the primary evidence custodian Deputy Jon

Williams or Deputy Kegley who was assigned as the secondary after Cundiff was removed. Major Hancock was certain Cundiff had turned in only a key card to Sheriff Speck when he was removed as custodian.

Despite what has been documented here, as of December 2023, Investigator Cundiff was still working as a deputy for the sheriff's office and was the lead detective in the Faubush-Norfleet murder case, detailed later in this book.

Documented on August 17, 2022, in Detective Keeton's report, "Detective Keeton also discussed with Sheriff Speck the issues with the missing and recently located master evidence key. The evidence key had gone missing after Bland resigned on October 15, 2020. The unknown whereabouts of the key was the reason that Deputy Jon Williams had the lock replaced on January 14, 2021 (Memorandum dated February 26, 2021). Until it was discovered in the pool car, no one could account for the missing key."

It was also documented that, "Deputy Williams agreed that if someone accessed the evidence room with the master key, it would allow access to the unsecured key box. The key box access would allow access to the keys that bypassed the coded doors to the gun vault door and wall locker."

In other words, it appears that from October 2020 until August 2022 (almost two years), no one in authority knew where the master key to the evidence room was located. Anyone could have had access to the evidence room, and there was no process for tracking this all-important master key to the Pulaski County Sheriff's Office evidence room. Such a lack of accountability is astonishing given the momentous importance of a secure evidence room.

Again, this happens while no one is watching.

On September 19, 2022, there was a hearing before Pulaski Circuit Judge Teresa Whitaker regarding the missing evidence/currency. I was notified a day or so prior to this hearing, so I personally attended it. This hearing was requested by two criminal defense attorneys with pending criminal cases in Pulaski County. These cases would have had evidence that was handled by the Pulaski County evidence room during the time frame of the missing evidence and currency, as with the Faubush-Norfleet murder case. The point being, if an evidence room is this messed up and riddled with suspicion, how can any evidence from this evidence room be trusted to use in any criminal case? These attorneys were demanding that KSP Detective Keeton's report be turned over in full to them, and rightfully so. No citizen should be subjected to the possibility of a long prison sentence based on conceivably tainted evidence.

Keeton's investigation into the missing evidence/currency would be considered Brady material in any criminal case that involved evidence from this unsecure evidence room. The concept of Brady material originates from the US Supreme Court case, Brady v. Maryland. The best definition I've seen that defines Brady material is by the Legal Information Institute at Cornell Law School:

> Brady material is derived from the United States Supreme Court case Brady v. Maryland in 1963. It established a rule that the prosecution has a constitutional duty of due process to disclose material evidence favorable to a defendant. In practice, if the prosecutor suppresses or fails to disclose evidence that is material to the defendant's guilt verdict or sentence, or influences the "credibility of a witness," no matter whether the prosecution is of good or bad faith, intentionally or inadvertently, the defendant can use the Brady material to get a new trial.

While Brady deals with exculpatory evidence, impeachment evidence is addressed by another US Supreme Court case, Giglio v. United States. Under Giglio, the government has a duty to disclose impeachment information relating to government witnesses. Being a judge that adheres to the rule of law, Judge Whitaker did the right thing and granted the hearing.

Judge Whitaker placed KSP Detective Keeton under oath, and defense attorneys began firing questions. Keeton kept refusing to answer questions, stating the matter was still an ongoing investigation. The defense attorneys were becoming frustrated when Judge Whitaker stepped in and began asking questions. One of the key questions Judge Whitaker asked Detective Keeton: "Was there any other evidence missing other than the currency?" Detective Keeton responded with no. Then Judge Whitaker asked, "How do you know this?" And Keeton answered, "Because of the audit." Now keep in mind this was the audit that also documented other evidence, not just money, was missing. Then she asked, "Who conducted the audit?" Detective Keeton answered, "The Pulaski County Sheriff's Office did an internal audit." In this back and forth between Judge Whitaker and Detective Keeton, it was revealed that from 2015 to November 2021, there were no real audits or inspections conducted on the evidence room. Further, the only audits ever conducted were internal audits by the sheriff's office. There were no audits or inspections of any kind from an outside, objective agency on record for the sheriff's office until Detective Keeton's investigation. I would later learn, to my surprise, that this lack of outside, objective inspections of evidence rooms in Kentucky is somehow very normal.

The fact that Keeton referred to these internal audits, under oath in this hearing, means he knew about these audits and either lied to Judge Whitaker about missing evidence other than money, or he knew about the existence of the other audits and did no real investigation into them, therefore glossing over the other missing evidence. If Detective Keeton had actually investigated these audits, he should have found the memos and pages and pages of missing evidence, not just the currency, as he told Judge Whitaker. Again, much like the issue with Somerset City Attorney John Adams and leachate, either this was gross incompetence, never corrected memory lapse, or a potential outright perjury by Detective Keeton to Judge Whitaker.

Many questions have to be ascertained from this case, one of which is where was the oversight of Detective Keeton's investigation? Did he not have a KSP supervisor closely following this important investigation? Any supervisor with half a brain would have seen these pitfalls ahead of time and should have properly advised the investigator on the proper steps to take during this investigation. After submitting an ORR to the KSP, they produced no documents indicating any type of supervision of this investigator. Further, where was the prosecutor's office and their oversight? In very important cases like this one, the prosecutor's office should absolutely be following the progress of the investigator, and the investigator should have been keeping the prosecutor informed every step of the way. It is the prosecutor's job to give at least some oversight of the investigation in order to give guidance on legal issues. Apparently this too never happened. It appears the only real checks and balances on this case was in fact Judge Whitaker.

It must be noted that, in my humble opinion, previous judges in Pulaski County would have never even granted this hearing much less made the KSP turn over this report. Against a mountain of objections from the Commonwealth Attorney David Dalton, Judge Whitaker did the right thing. She followed the law and made Detective Keeton turn over his report. To this day, I firmly believe that Judge Whitaker may be the saving grace of Pulaski County. The best legal results are obtained when cases are presented by ethical attorneys before truly impartial judges brave enough to follow the law, not politics.

In early October 2022, I received a call from a confidential source that the Pulaski County Sheriff's Office had lost a narcotics dog training kit in Wayne County, Kentucky. I was told it was found as a result of a narcotics search warrant at a suspected drug house in Wayne County. In October 2022, the Wayne County Sheriff's Office publicized a report that, it had seized a black box containing K-9 training narcotics. This K-9 training kit was believed to have been lost by another agency. The Wayne County sheriff did not release which agency the kit came from. I sent the Wayne County Sheriff's Office and the Pulaski County Sheriff's Office ORRs. Both refused to answer, stating that it was "under investigation." As of December 2023, there are still no answers to this major debacle. Keep in mind that these narcotics kits are supposed to be controlled by the DEA, as they actually contain small amounts of narcotics. They are supposed to be properly logged in and out of, in this case, the Pulaski County evidence room. This didn't happen, and the kit ended up in a drug house, only located after the execution of an unrelated search warrant.

Again, this happens while no one is watching.

This concerned me greatly that an evidence room could go un-inspected for years and have no real outside, objective inspections by an overseeing agency. I began to do some research and found that no evidence room in Kentucky is required by law or regulation to have outside, objective, random inspections of any kind. Kentucky's evidence rooms are simply allowed to operate with only in-house inspections. This means they get to police themselves, exclusively. Now what could possibly go wrong here? I then found other cases in Kentucky where things went horribly wrong with the lack of evidence room oversight. This prompted me to write the following article, publish it, and read it on the *Truth or Politics* show.

Are Kentucky's Evidence Rooms the "Wild, Wild West" of the Criminal Justice Process?
OP.ED. By: Darlene F. Price
TRUTH or POLITICS

The fictional character Sherlock Holmes was often quoted as saying, "follow the money." This of course was based upon a long established assumption that one could actually follow a chain of evidence, a money trail that would lead Holmes to discover the bad guy. But what if that all important evidence was then tainted or lost once it reached the all important evidence room? What then?

Decades of analysis, research, investigation, instruction and U.S. Supreme Court case law have centered on this very thing, the proper collection and storage of evidence surrounding criminal cases. Entire bachelor degrees at prestigious universities have centered on "chain of custody" and evidence collection. Law schools have literally hours and hours dedicated to the importance of this area of law. Moreover, there are literally five (5) hit television shows that center on "Crime Scene Investigation—CSI."

Why, one should ask, is this topic so important? The simplest of answers are: so that the innocent go free and the guilty are made to answer. When the chain of custody of criminal evidence cannot be trusted, the order of a "fair and just" system is most certainly under attack, and the results are nothing less than dangerous; dangerous for the innocently accused and dangerous for victims of crimes.

Recently in Kentucky it has become very apparent that there are little to no checks and balances on evidence rooms where this all important evidence is being stored. Careful research into the "Kentucky Rules of Evidence,""Kentucky Revised Statutes," the Kentucky League of Cities (KLC) and The Kentucky Association of Counties (KACO) yield that there are no real apparent laws or procedures that are MANDATED regarding the storage, conduct and oversight of Kentucky's evidence rooms after evidence has been admitted to said rooms. There are no laws or regulations requiring that an outside, independent agency conduct routine, surprise audits of Kentucky's evidence rooms.

In December 2019, three Kentucky State Police commanding officers filed a Whistleblower lawsuit against the state and department claiming they were retaliated against for reporting that troopers were stealing evidence from property rooms, seized from criminal cases (see WDBR.com article: https://www.wdrb.com/in-depth/

kentucky-state-police-troopers-claim-fellow-officers-stole-evidence/ article_5b97bdca-1d17-11ea-913a-e32f4bda7c11.html).

A Jury in this lawsuit awarded the three troopers $900K in this Whistleblower case (https://www.wdrb.com/jury-awards-3-ksp-troopers-900k-in-whistleblower-case/article_40e7150c-8b97-11ec-993a-335daaf914fd.html).

Just in one county alone, Pulaski County, Kentucky, it has come to light that evidence rooms controlled by the Pulaski County Sheriff's Department (PCSD) and the Somerset Police Department (SPD) have been easily breached, and evidence gone missing.

In the PCSD alone since 2015, pages of evidence and currency have gone missing in numerous criminal cases. This missing evidence involves, but is not limited to, the following: Approximately $25,000.00 dollars, drugs, DNA evidence, weapons, ammunition, spent rounds, and several computers/ laptops, just to name a few. Also discovered in the Kentucky State Police investigation that followed, was the fact that the "master key" to the evidence room had been missing and for how long, no one knows.

What followed in the discovery of this missing evidence was nothing short of shocking. Through information gained from confidential sources and an actual evidence hearing on this very discovery, it was exposed by TRUTH or POLITICS that the PCSD evidence room had no type of audit for at least 5 years. Then only when an outsider discovered the missing currency did an audit show that there was much more missing evidence than just currency. A much larger problem that was painfully disclosed in this same hearing was the fact that NO ONE from any objective outside agency was conducting the audits of the PCSD evidence room. The PCSD for years was simply allowed to audit and inspect themselves with absolutely no oversight. Further, it was found that even though the PCSD evidence room had video surveillance, the surveillance recordings (also evidence) was not properly retained and stored to be used by the investigator to ascertain who and how this evidence went missing. To date this case has been conveniently closed, no one has been fired and no one is going to jail.

This prompted me to question evidence procedures and the handling of evidence in other evidence lockers across the state of Kentucky. Just as I was diving into this readily apparent problem and only weeks after the PCSD missing evidence was exposed, yet another incident in this same county demonstrated yet another breach of security in the SPD evidence room. Apparently, a newly retired SPD captain was the target of a Kentucky State Police search warrant at his residence in Pulaski County Kentucky. This warrant was allegedly based upon an actual video of said captain entering the temporary evidence room located in City Hall, with unauthorized keys and removing evidence. The warrant allegedly yielded the finding of a stolen weapon, and suspected drugs. The good news here is at least this evidence room had video surveillance that the investigators could use to potentially prosecute the Captain.

A search of "Kentucky Revised Statutes" (KRS) and administrative rules and regulations in Kentucky have yielded little actual laws, regulations or objective enforcement from any outside auditing agency regarding evidence rooms in Kentucky. For the most part, evidence rooms all across the state are simply allowed to escape any type of objective, outside, oversight or audits. Much like PCSD, they are simply allowed to audit themselves, or worse yet, escape audit of any type for years on end. I found this to be a most disturbing discovery. What this means is, that when police officers testify before grand juries and at preliminary hearings, their testimony regarding this all important chain of custody and storing of evidence is just blindly accepted as pure and trustworthy.

I wonder how many "true bills" would be handed down by grand juries if they knew ahead of time that evidence rooms could be compromised and evidence not only gone missing, but potentially altered for prosecution? Surely in severely compromised evidence rooms like PCSD one must wonder what else has transpired, like altering evidence or making evidence disappear in order to falsely release suspects or convict suspects in criminal cases. This is a fair question. This is a question that the state of Kentucky law makers and administrators must quickly find an answer to in order to restore faith in the criminal justice system in Kentucky. This is exactly how innocent people go to jail, and the guilty may walk free. Again, I cannot express just how dangerous this gaping black hole in our criminal justice system actually is.

Honest cops who work diligently to properly collect and process criminal evidence will suffer when it is exposed in the system that the overall security of said evidence may be compromised by a sloppy, negligently run evidence room.

Moreover, suspects who cannot afford the best, expensive criminal defense attorneys are often times at a severe disadvantage. The element of time is not on their side. These suspects will be assigned a "Public Defender" who, often times, is overwhelmed with too many cases. They simply don't have the time to carefully review or have investigators dig into these types of cases where the chain of custody of evidence is paramount to any case. There are very good, honest, and hard working public defenders. However, it has been well established that public defenders more often than not do not have the funding or time to do what high paid, criminal defense attorneys and firms can do. Recently, a phrase has been coined, "You're better off being guilty and rich, than being innocent and poor."

A case in point is the infamous O.J. Simpson murder case. O.J. Simpson walked free primarily because he could afford the "dream team" of the best of the best criminal defense attorneys. What happened in that case has now been studied and analyzed by jurisprudence all across the field of criminal justice. These attorneys had the time and assets to investigate and pick apart the prosecution's case. I am familiar with this case and the Los Angeles Police Department's evidence procedures because I worked as a Special Agent for many years on cases with the LAPD. This evidence room, unlike the PCSD, actually had routine, objective, outside audits and oversight by the State Attorney General's Office. Despite this oversight, holes in procedures were brought to light and a well respected police detective who was the "finder" (collector) of most of the evidence in this case, was exposed as a perjurer. Defense attorneys will forever use the coined phrase, "we need to Mark Fuhrman the evidence." This dream team was able to "Mark Fuhrman" the evidence in this case because they had the man-power, the time and the assets to do so. This is NOT what most defendants face when they are entering the criminal justice system. Juries must rely on face value that the police officers and evidence rooms are as pristine as they always seem to testify to.

As we now have discovered, crucial evidence may be in jeopardy in Kentucky. There is no requirement that a real outside agency that conducts routine audits and inspections on evidence rooms in Kentucky. There are no statutes that require this. Perhaps this is why we have not one, but two embarrassing incidents of breach of evidence in just one county here in Kentucky.

I have personally verified that at least five (5) criminal defense attorneys were actually shocked to learn this. This means that previous criminal cases may have gone unchecked and evidence rooms unchallenged by defense attorneys who reasonably assumed that evidence rooms and the collection of evidence had better checks and balances in the state of Kentucky.

So, what is the answer? The answer to me is obvious; our state legislature has to come up with reasonable laws that require routine, outside, objective inspections and audits of evidence rooms all across the state of Kentucky. This agency can either be controlled or run by either the State Attorney General's Office or the Kentucky State Auditor's office. This newly formed inspection team must only have the responsibility of inspection, oversight and control of evidence rooms. This is way too important to sparse out this responsibility to an agency that is already handling numerous other types of inspections. This is the only way to ensure that crucial evidence is being collected, stored and conveyed at trial as the police officers and prosecutors now portray—that really isn't happening. Anything short of this lends itself to not only a great gaping hole in criminal justice, but it also lends itself to compromising the very law enforcement officers who are charged with protecting us from this great gaping hole.

> Darlene F. Price, J.D.
> Ex. Producer & Host of **TRUTH** or **POLITICS**
> Author: "Bordergate, the story the government doesn't want you to read."

After this article was published and read out loud on my *Truth or Politics* show, I was contacted by several defense attorneys who were interested in the lack of controls in evidence rooms in Kentucky. I was shocked by the fact that many defense attorneys simply assumed that evidence rooms in Kentucky had some sort of outside, objective oversight when in actuality, they do not. I also sent this article to the Kentucky attorney general's office and to several of our state legislatures. As of January 2025, nothing has been done to solve this glaring, serious problem. Why is this important, you ask? Simply stated, this type of gross mishandling of evidence rooms is exactly how innocent people can end up in prison and the guilty go free.

In May 2024, the Kentucky Court of Appeals reversed the jury's decision regarding the three Kentucky state troopers who won their whistleblower lawsuit. This suit was based on the extreme retaliation they received from their leadership for exposing the fact that cops were stealing evidence from KSP evidence rooms. This decision rates as one of the worst decisions I have ever read. This reversal has now set a very dangerous precedent—it is acceptable for law enforcement managers in the Commonwealth of Kentucky to silence any officer who dares to expose corruption in any form. If I had a Jackass award, I would certainly give it to the judges who made this decision. Moreover, it provides a judicial seal of approval that Kentucky's evidence rooms are open for business to any corrupt cop who wants to steal or even alter evidence in criminal cases.

The question is why? Why would this court of appeals do this? The only real answer I can surmise is perhaps they are protecting the system that got them elected. The other question is why were there no prosecutions for these thefts from KSP evidence rooms? Where was the serious criminal investigation into these KSP officers' allegations of evidence being stolen? Further, why would anyone trust KSP to be the investigative agency on other evidence room failures and missing evidence when it apparently cannot or does not properly control its own evidence rooms?

On January 15, 2024, former Somerset Police Captain Michael Correll pleaded guilty to twenty-two counts, after being caught removing evidence from the Somerset Police Department evidence room. These counts included third-degree burglary, tampering with physical evidence, abuse of the public trust, theft by unlawful taking, trafficking in a controlled substance, receiving stolen property, official misconduct, and unlawful access to a computer. I find it interesting that this evidence room is located not only in Pulaski County but also at Somerset city hall, in the same building as Mayor Keck's office.

After Captain Correll's retirement, he was somehow allowed to keep possession of police department keys and key cards, apparently giving him access to virtually everything within the department, including the evidence room. The fact that there were no checks and balances to sign back in with these keys and cards is beyond amazing—and not in a good way. What should have happened with proper evidence room procedures is that any officer should have been required to sign for any property they were issued, including any keys or key cards. There should have been a sheet, computerized or printed, that served as a receipt with a complete list and precise inventory of everything the officer was issued, with his signature and date. Then an out-processing procedure should have occurred wherein a supervisor oversaw everything the officer returned when he was processed out of the department. If he failed to return any item, there should have been immediate action taken to investigate and document these missing items, especially keys and key cards to evidence rooms. This case is precisely why out-processing and in-processing procedures are so very important to properly keep track of property that has been issued to that officer. Apparently this was not done or at least no one checked it.

Some of what Captain Correll stole from the evidence room were methamphetamine, and other, pills. A subsequent audit indicated that over 8,500 pills were missing from the evidence room. He reportedly used the entry cards to access a police computer without consent. This is what he was caught doing. The real question is how much more did he get away with before he was caught? This guy had pretty much un-limited access to the evidence room, secure information, and property, and much like the Pulaski County sheriff's evidence room, there was very little oversight or checks and balances. While no one's watching, the fox can clean out the chicken coop. Again, as stated in the above article, this is a real problem throughout Kentucky because there are no real regulations or laws requiring outside, independent, regular audits or inspections of Kentucky's evidence rooms.

On February 29, 2024, after a very long sentencing hearing (five hours), Mike Correll was sentenced to five years in prison. He will be eligible for parole in 2025.

During my research, numerous interviews, and my work as a crim-inal defense investigator for attorneys in Kentucky, I came to understand some very disturbing things about local and county law enforcement. Many times the first officers on the scene would have no real evidence kits or all of the necessary items to even begin to properly process a crime scene. Many had no fingerprint kits, no ability to collect gunshot residue (GSR), no plaster cast material to collect shoe imprints, and some did not even have a basic tape measure and proper recording devices. Many were using their cell phones for photographic evidence instead of good camera equipment and video. Very few had body cameras (body cams), and the ones who had access to them were simply allowed to refuse to wear them.

Even more disturbing was the lack of proper training and experience many of these officers who were attempting to process these crime scenes had. In one 2024case (not in Pulaski County), there was a two-vehicle traffic accident where the victim driver was not expected to survive. The importance of properly processing a potential vehicular homicide scene cannot be emphasized enough. The female victim actually lived through this horrible accident, but the first officers at the scene would not know this until much later. The *Reader's Digest* version of this is that an intoxicated driver veered into the female victim's lane of travel, striking her vehicle.

This was by anyone's description a very complicated crime scene and potential vehicle homicide. This should have been processed by the most competent, trained, and experienced officers. In fact, there should have been at least three officers processing this crime scene. That is not what happened. Two officers responded to this accident. One of them was basically a volunteer officer with the title of special deputy, and the other was a sheriff's sergeant. The special deputy had some former air force security and dog handler experience but certainly no extensive crime scene investigation training and experience. The sergeant had only the basic crime scene training that is taught at local police academies. This basic training does not rise to the level of the extensive training and experience one would need to possess in order to properly complete such a consequential crime scene investigation. Even if both of them had remained at this scene, they should have asked for assistance from a more experienced and trained crime scene investigator. This too did not happen.

Again, let me reiterate—you only get one shot at a crime scene. It is my understanding that a KSP officer did respond and was waived off by the two lesser trained deputies. Then the unthinkable happened: the sergeant left the special deputy alone to process this scene himself and responded to a much less important call. This was a Charlie Foxtrot of gargantuan proportions. Needless to say this crime scene was botched, and I'm being kind when I say botched. This lone deputy attempted a very complicated traffic accident investigation that could very well have turned into a vehicular homicide and made glaring mistakes. These mistakes were so flagrant that the commonwealth's attorney may not be able to prosecute the case.

The prosecutor in this case now has an almost impossible task of bringing the appropriate charges because of not only the botched crime scene but also the lack of a proper follow-up investigation. In my humble opinion, the sheriff sergeant who left this crime scene for a much lesser call should have been either fired for this glaring blunder or at least demoted and punished in some way. This too apparently did not happen.

Unfortunately there are sometimes turf wars between agencies and between the state police and local law enforcement. I feel this is the reason why many times the locals who do not have the proper training, experience, equipment, and resources to process these crime scenes properly will not accept help from either the KSP or federal law enforcement.

This story is not an isolated incident. Beginning with my *BorderGate* story over the past twenty-five years, I have either been directly involved with or have investigated numerous events like the ones being documented in this book. Too many of these investigations start and end with the police completely botching criminal investigations. Some involve federal investigators refusing to investigate at all, despite clear evidence that they should be stepping in. Too many of them involve some sort of cover-up of the botched investigation because of what may appear to be bruised egos, turf wars, incompetence, laziness, or politics at play.

What people need to understand is that these botched investigations, no matter what the reason, are not rare in Kentucky. They are quite common. In almost every case I have investigated, either as a defense investigator or investigative journalist, I have easily found numerous flaws. I have also uncovered that many of the so-called experts (ballistics, medical examiners, etc.) mostly located at the Frankfort, Kentucky, labs, were also lacking in their techniques, proper protocols, and outside, independent oversight. Occasionally the flaws I see percolate up in reported appellate cases.

Again, I cannot stress enough that many of these huge mistakes could have been prevented if there had been some sort of outside peer group and objective, procedural oversight in place. The experts need to have protocols that include outside, objective oversight of their work—not just their rank-and-file supervisors or people in their chain of command. The only things that prevent positive change to these incredible deficiencies are pride and arrogance of public officials who could step in and make these necessary changes.

Meanwhile, the victims and their families of these botched investigations are rarely in any way compensated for how they were treated, even after the deficiencies are exposed. There are no apologies and never anyone to admit to the wrongdoing. In these cases the victims are victimized twice.

In Kentucky, it is extremely hard to file suit against any public official or police department because of the sovereign immunity laws that exist. These laws are to protect public officials and not the public, even though the courts and politicians claim otherwise. They prevent holding anyone accountable, even with serious infractions—oftentimes no matter what the evidence shows. These types of cases are so difficult to bring to trial that most experienced and competent attorneys will not touch them.

Knowing this type of immunity exists creates an atmosphere of impunity for both public officials and police. They know full well what they can get away with while no one's watching.

The following chapter serves as an example of precisely why we must have proper oversight and routine inspections of police evidence rooms, utilizing outside, objective sources, not just self-inspections. This chapter also serves to demonstrate why we must have competent management of high-profile investigations. Please remember as you read this next chapter that investigators only get one shot at a crime scene.

Chapter 6

MURDER ON FAUBUSH–NORFLEET ROAD: IT WAS A DARK AND STORMY NIGHT

When processing a crime scene with a deceased body, sometimes investigators lose sight that the dead are people who have a story to tell. That most important story is about what happened to them and the fact that they can no longer tell their story. No matter the life they lived, they still deserve to have the right person held accountable. The only way to get that story now is from the crime scene. If investigators look hard enough and take the time to ask the right questions in the correct manner, investigators can find that story and speak for the dead. Isn't that what the deceased and their families deserve? Isn't that what we all should want if it were one of our loved ones lying there on the floor? Never forget, witnesses and suspects may lie but properly obtained evidence does not. Moreover, the smallest thing in a crime scene that you may think is most insignificant will sometimes be the very clue that assists in solving the case. Oftentimes what you think you have isn't at all what is true.

In early April 2021, I received a call from my favorite criminal defense attorney, Jim Cox. Attorney Cox and I had worked two prior murder cases and two drug cases together. In each of these cases, our clients went home. Some of that was due to my investigation, but most of this was due to the excellent work of Jim Cox, a seasoned, cunning defense attorney. To say that Jim is an interesting character is an understatement. At first glance, Jim comes across as an unassuming, good ol' country boy. He is very low-key and seemingly unimpressive—until he cross-examines someone on the stand. He is an absolute genius at meticulously picking apart witnesses on the stand. Then, in closing arguments, Jim is nothing short of a wizard at hitting home runs in front of juries.

Jim retired from the Kentucky Department of Public Advocacy's (DPA) office and then went into private practice. Jim Cox is the primary reason that my husband, Austin Price, is such an excellent attorney. Austin worked under Jim's expert tutelage at the DPA before he went into private practice and subsequently became the McCreary County attorney (prosecutor). Further, as well educated and experienced as I thought I was as an investigator, I still learned so very much from Jim Cox in these cases. If not *the* best, Jim Cox is most certainly one of the best criminal defense attorneys I have had the opportunity to work with in all of my almost forty years as an investigator for prosecution and defense.

Jim requested that we team up again for another murder case, and I immediately accepted. Not only is it an honor to work with Jim, but it is also a joy to work with such an honest and professional person. Jim had already heard about what I had uncovered on the Pulaski County sheriff's evidence room. I drove to Jim's office the next day and provided him with a copy of KSP Detective Michael Keeton's report on the evidence room investigation. Then I began to pick apart the investigation, or lack thereof, on the Faubush-Norfleet Road murder case.

The Faubush-Norfleet murder case was a real whodunit in every sense. The suspects in this case were the residents who lived at this mobile home: Ronald Baker, James (name changed), and Beth (name changed).

Ronald Baker's son, Samuel Baker (our client), did not live at the mobile home / crime scene and was also a suspect. The victim found at the scene was Clarence Roberts (name changed). This case begins on March 18, 2021, when the Pulaski County 911 center received a call regarding a shooting on Faubush-Norfleet Road in Pulaski, County, Kentucky.

Please keep in mind that this was just days after Investigator Cody Cundiff was scheduled for an interrogation and polygraph regarding the missing currency/evidence from the sheriff's office evidence room, where Investigator Cundiff was an evidence custodian. Despite this cloud hanging over Investigator Cundiff 's head, he was dispatched to this murder scene, as was Deputy Bobby Jones (later elected Sheriff Jones). In this Faubush-Norfleet murder case, all residents of this crime scene (Ronald, Samuel, James and Beth) were in fact viable witnesses or suspects who should have also been treated as key suspects in this case, until properly ruled out, but this did not happen.

As anyone who has ever watched an episode of *Matlock*, *Justified*, or *CSI* would know, just because someone dials 911 and reports a shooting, that person is not eliminated as a suspect. My memory takes me immediately back to the highly publicized Susan Smith child murder case. To refresh your memory, on October 25, 1994, in South Carolina, a crying Susan Smith was found on the doorstep of a residence claiming she had been carjacked and that her sons, three-year-old Michael and fourteen-month-old Alex, were kidnapped during the crime. For nine days, she and the children's father pleaded with the press for the safe return of their sons. What happened then was what one would call real police work.

The officers in the Susan Smith case did what they were supposed to do and did not assume that Susan was an innocent victim. They actually separated her, took her to the police station, and interrogated her. They did several follow-up interviews as they developed information in the case. The cops did a thorough crime scene investigation at Susan's home and where the kids were allegedly kidnapped. One of the items of evidence they found was a letter Smith had received from Tom Findlay—a man she was having a relationship with. Findlay did not want the responsibility of a ready-made family; he also was not convinced that their different backgrounds and Susan's behavior toward other men were suitable for a committed relationship. He sent her a Dear John letter of sorts explaining all this in October 1994. The investigators found this letter, which brought even more scrutiny on what Smith had told the police thus far.

The investigators conducted several interviews in which Smith would change her story several times. She also took several polygraph tests and all were inconclusive. After nine days of good old-fashioned investigative police and CSI work, Smith confessed to killing her own children.

That is *not* what happened in the Faubush-Norfleet murder case.

To begin, it was in fact a cold, dark, and stormy night on Faubush-Norfleet Road. This shooting took place in a rural location at a mobile home in Pulaski County. The renter of the mobile home was a drug addict, former drug dealer, and convicted felon named Ronald Baker. Ronald Baker, by his own admission, had done six years in prison for drug dealing. The victim in this case, Clarence Roberts (name changed), was found in Ronald Baker's rented mobile home, shot three times. At the time of the shooting, Roberts was out on bond on a drug-related burglary case. From the body cameras worn by the sheriff deputies in this case, it appears that this was perhaps some sort of drug deal gone bad. There were methamphetamine pipes and drug paraphernalia all over this place. To state that this mobile home was in disarray would be an understatement.

In our follow-up investigation, there had been at least twelve previous calls to 911 involving some sort of domestic violence, complaints of theft, or firearms being discharged at this mobile home involving suspect Ronald Baker. Each and every time the officers would respond, not much initial investigation or follow-up was done. My interviews of neighbors clearly painted a picture that this was a drug house and Ronald Baker was back to his drug dealing ways, despite being on probation. The fact that this shooting takes place in this atmosphere is not surprising.

This case was initiated by a 911 call from suspect/witness Ronald Baker. Here's the actual transcript of the 911 call from Ronald Baker:

911 OPERATOR: 911, what's your emergency?

RONALD BAKER: Ah, it's Ronald Baker I need a, I need an ambulance here and [inaudible], out here at 910, 19 [inaudible] road.

911: 910 Faubush-Norfleet Road?

RB: Yes, my son has been here again [pause, breathing hard].

911: He's what?

RB: My son's been here again.

911: Okay, what's going on that you need an ambulance?

RB: [breathing heavily, footsteps and voices in the background] I need an ambulance too, I need an ambulance right away.

911: Okay, what's—

RB: He's shot, he's shot. He shot somebody.

911: He shot somebody?

RB: Yes he did, hurry! Please hurry!

911: Okay, we got them on the way.

RB: [inaudible] Oh my god! Oh!

911: Who else is there?

RB: [inaudible] Clarence Roberts, Clarence Roberts that he shot. Oh god.

911: Your son just shot Clarence Roberts?

RB: Yes, he just did, yeah. Oh my god.

911: Who are you talk—let me talk to who else is there.

RB: Nobody else is here. Hey, come on, hurry.

911: Okay, we got them on the way. What's your name?

RB: Ronald Baker.

911: Earl Baker?

RB: Yeah. Please hurry.

911: Okay. What's your son's name? [dial tone, then numerous ringtones]

RB: [inaudible] Oh my god.

911: Ronald Baker.

RB: [Crying]

911: All right, is there somebody else with you?

RB: No, nobody else is here with me.

911: Okay, where's your son at?

RB: He just took off back down the road, I don't know what he's driving.

911: Okay, what, what's your son's name?

RB: Samuel Baker. He's in a loud car, I know that much, it's loud. [inaudible] he won't get up.

911: And he's inside the house?

RB: Yes he's [inaudible] inside the house.

911: Okay. Where was Samuel going?

RB: [inaudible] he's coming back.

911: Who's that female I hear talking?

RB: Ain't no, it's the TV, ma'am.

911: It's the TV?

RB: Yes, ma'am.

911: Okay. Who hung up the phone just a minute ago?

RB: Nobody hung up no phone, ma'am.

911: Okay.

RB: That was call waiting [inaudible] call me, I ain't answering it.

911: Okay. Where did he shoot him in, at?

RB: [Inaudible] in the chest, in the chest looks like. He's not saying nothing, he ain't moving [inaudible]. Oh my god. I see blood.

911: Okay, can you go see if he's breathing?

RB: Yeah, he's breathing right now. Hey, Clarence. Hey, Clarence. I feel a heartbeat. Yeah, I feel a heartbeat. He's alive.

911: Is he breathing?

RB: Yeah, I, I can't tell, I can't tell. He's laying face down.

911: Okay, is there any way you can turn him over?

RB: [inaudible] I don't, I can't, I [inaudible] have to move everything here. [inaudible] I don't want to turn him on his back, dude.

911: Yeah, go ahead and turn him on his back.

RB: [inaudible] let me try. Oh my god, I can't. Oh, shit far.

911: Anna, go ahead and send fire.

RB: Oh, I'm [inaudible]. He has a big hole, oh my god. Please come here. Please.

911: Okay, we got someone on the way.

RB: [inaudible yelling]

911: Do you know what—

RB: [inaudible yelling]

911: What kind of gun did he shoot him with?

RB: Ah, I don't think he's, oh my god.

911: Did he shoot him with a handgun or a rifle?

RB: In the belly. Oh god!

911: Okay. All right, we've got them on the way, okay.

RB: [inaudible] Oh my god. Oh my god.

911: All right, we got them on the way, okay. And you think he is still breathing?

RB: Oh my god.

911: Brittney, did you send fire?

RB: [inaudible] Oh my god. Ma'am.

911: Okay, hang on just a second, okay?

RB: [inaudible]

911: Okay, we got everybody on the way out to you, okay?

RB: Oh god.

911: Okay, do you have, do you have anything you can try and control the bleeding on his chest?

RB: Oh god.

911: How bad is he bleeding?

RB: Oh my god.

911: Mr. Baker.

RB: Oh god. Oh shit.

911: Can you take, how bad is he bleeding?

RB: Oh god. Hell man. Hello.

911: He doesn't know. He just says it's loud.

RB: Huh? Hello.

911: Mr. Baker.

RB: Yes.

911: Can you tell me how bad he's bleeding?

RB: [inaudible] he's bled to death, I think. He's not alive, he's not breathing now. His heartbeat's quit.

911: So you don't think he's bled, do you think you can do CPR?

RB: No. Oh honey, I don't know how to do that.

911: I can tell you how.

RB: There's blood everywhere.

911: Okay.

RB: Oh my god. Oh.

911: Where does your son live?

RB: I don't know where he lives. I don't have no idea. He's been out here the other night with a gun threaten me, and he come here tonight and shot him.

911: Okay. Does, does, ah, Clarence live there with you?

RB: [inaudible] loud car, little bitty loud car.

911: Little bitty loud car? Do you know what color it is?

RB: No. Oh.

911: Does Clarence live with you?

RB: No, he does not, he just come out to visit.

911: He just come to visit.

RB: Yeah.

911: Okay.

RB: I locked the door, okay.

911: Okay.

RB: [inaudible] coming back.

911: I'll let you know when they're, when they're on the way, okay. Had your son been drinking or doing drugs?

RB: Oh, he was doing drugs the other day. Okay.

911: You know what he does?

RB: Oh my god.

911: Do you, do you know what kind of drugs he does?

RB: He does meth. [inaudible]

911: [inaudible] okay.

RB: Oh my god. Oh. Oh shit.

911: I've got them on the way. Are you okay? He didn't hurt you?

RB: No, he didn't hurt me.

911: Okay, I know you're upset. Were they arguing or did he just shoot him for no reason?

RB: He just, he, I asked him to leave, okay, I said just leave and he needed just a few more days to calm down over what he did to me the other day, and I said [inaudible]. I said I can't take it, you got to go. And then I said I'm gonna go on to bed, okay. I said you need to leave, and then I walked back to the bedroom and laid down and the next thing I heard was gun shots. And I come in here and he's laying on the floor and my son's [inaudible].

911: Okay. But you don't see your son outside anywhere?

RB: [inaudible]

911: His car's gone?

RB: He's gone, yeah.

911: Okay.

RB: Loud.

911: Okay. And you don't know where he lives?

RB: He lives with his mom, Jessica Toomy (name changed), his mom is married to Rob Toomy (name changed).

911: Rob Toomy. How old's your son?

RB: Twenty-one, twenty, twenty-one. Oh.

911: Okay.

RB: Oh boy. Oh god.

911: Okay, is Earl your first name?

RB: Ah, Ronald. Ronald Baker.

911: Okay.

RB: Yeah, Ronald Baker. Oh my god.

911: Okay, we've got everybody on the way. Okay.

RB: [inaudible] my son. [inaudible]

911: Okay, you got your doors all locked, right?

RB: Mmm hmm. God, god almighty. Oh god.

911: Was that on the fourteenth that he threatened you before?

RB: [inaudible]

911: All right.

RB: Oh my [inaudible]. My god.

911: Okay, hang on just a second. Okay.

RB: Oh. Oh my god. Oh my god.

The above typed words do not do this actual call justice. When I listened to this call, several times, I must say it sounded very disturbing.

To a layperson or a naive juror, Ronald Baker's performance could be believable. Unfortunately, crocodile tears often work, especially when they are not followed up with a competent investigation by the police.

When I discussed the case with attorney Jim Cox, I asked him if he had reviewed the body cams. Jim stated there weren't any. The prosecutor, David Dalton, had supposedly turned over any and all evidence in this case, and there were no body cameras. I knew from my confidential sources that the Pulaski County Sheriff's Office and the KSP did in fact provide body cams for their officers. I contacted my sources, and they told me that several of the deputies who had responded to the shooting at the Faubush-Norfleet crime scene that night did in fact wear body cams. I told Jim this, and he made another motion before the court for the sheriff's office to provide the body cams. And, once ordered by the judge, the body cams magically appeared. This would be the first of many appearances of attempting to hide evidence or delay our obtaining evidence that either the prosecution or the cops would engage in during this case.

On March 25, 2021, one week after the Faubush-Norfleet murder, Investigator Cundiff, the investigator assigned to this murder investigation, was relieved as evidence custodian by Major Hancock. This was after Investigator Cundiff was listed as a suspect on the KSP missing currency report and after he flunked a polygraph. Again, Investigator Cundiff knew he was going to be interrogated and polygraphed in this criminal investigation, before this shooting occurred. Investigator Cundiff was in fact listed in a KSP report as a suspect in the criminal case regarding the missing evidence. Certainly this would have weighed heavily on Investigator Cundiff's mind, not to mention that in any other department he would have been placed on administrative leave or, at the very least, riding a desk until the criminal investigation into missing evidence/currency had been concluded.

The Body Cameras

In viewing the body cameras of three different officers at the Faubush-Norfleet murder scene that night, I was amazed at what I saw. All three body cams were turned off almost at the same time. They all had an unknown gap of time before being turned back on. This should never have happened. What occurred during this gap? This can lead to suspicion as to what may have occurred while they were off. This would be a major topic of cross-examination by defendant Samuel Baker's attorney Jim Cox during the criminal trial that would take place three years later. The answers from the cops regarding the body cams being turned off were lackluster, to say the least. They had no legitimate explanations other than blaming the lack of rules or regulations against turning them off and that they allegedly had run out of storage for the data, which is unconvincing.

The second thing I noticed about the body cams was that one could use the video footage as a training tool as to how *not* to conduct a crime scene investigation. When the first deputy arrived and exited his vehicle, suspect Ronald Baker (the guy calling 911) was coming out of the mobile home. As Ronald Baker was stepping out of the home, I immediately noticed he had a large Buck knife on his belt and was no longer crying as he had been just minutes ago on the 911 call. Incidentally, this 911 call would be the only time Ronald Baker seems to cry over his friend, the victim, until his performance at the trial three years later.

The first officer on the scene listened to suspect Ronald Baker and that officer correctly kept Ronald Baker from going back into the residence until the investigator arrived. However, he failed to properly search Ronald Baker and allowed him to keep his knife. The appearance was that the officer just assumed Ronald Baker was not the shooter. Ronald Baker should have been patted down and placed in the back seat of the officer's cruiser until the investigator or person in charge arrived. This was not done. Ronald Baker was allowed to stand and walk around the crime scene unsupervised, where he could have done a number of things, including tamper with the evidence and manipulate the investigation. At one point he was allowed to go to a small shed, unsearched, unsupervised, to wait for the investigator. He could have had the murder weapon or spent rounds in his coat pockets, which were also not searched, and ample opportunity to toss this evidence anywhere, anytime he wanted.

Later in the investigation, the body cams show numerous people just standing around under an awning to the entrance of the home. You can see emergency personnel (EMS) step out of the doorway as they finished their unsuccessful lifesaving attempts on the victim. You can also see the coroner just standing around with the many officers and EMS personnel. At one point you can hear an officer actually say, "We have twelve people here." On another body cam, you can hear the officer say, "We're waiting on the investigator," which would have been Investigator Cundiff. The obvious problem with these videos is that the EMS personnel and others were just standing around in what would later be determined as the alleged crime scene area, stepping on possible evidence. Once it was determined that they could no longer save the victim, these EMS personnel, the coroner, and anyone else not assisting with the crime scene investigation should have been moved away from that area.

Some senior officer should have taken control of this scene until the investigator arrived. When the EMS personnel were finished, they should have been moved away from the potential crime scene in order to protect evidence. This never happened, even though Investigator Cundiff did not arrive until almost an hour later. That is a lot of time to have a crime scene uncontrolled and that many people walking all over it. Investigator Cundiff could have radioed ahead and instructed a senior officer to secure the scene until he arrived. At one point, you can see a state police trooper and Bobby Jones standing around and not doing much else. Investigator Cundiff could have enlisted them to help—this too was not done.

As everyone was standing around under the awning of the mobile home, suspect Ronald Baker kept trying to get back into the mobile home, where the dead body lay. Then you can see from the body cameras an EMS personnel step into the mobile home, reach over the dead body, and grab a coat that was laying on the island next to the body (a.k.a. the actual crime scene). The EMS person then gave the coat to suspect Ronald Baker, and Ronald Baker put the coat on and placed his hands in the pockets. Ronald Baker then walked to a shed behind the home, unsupervised by anyone. At no time during the crime scene investigation (or lack thereof) does anyone search Ronald Baker or his coat. If Ronald Baker had been properly detained in the police cruisers, then he would not have had reason to request a coat, an unforced error that occurred right in front of several cops standing there with Ronald Baker. Ronald Baker could have had anything in his pockets (e.g., spent rounds, a gun, drugs, etc.) and taken them to the shed where they may have been disposed. Ronald Baker also could have had spent rounds in his pockets and planted them in an area that benefitted him. The body cams clearly demonstrated that no one was really watching him or treating him as a possible suspect in this shooting.

Also seen from the body cams were numerous items of drugs and drug paraphernalia. There were several meth pipes, needles, and what appeared to be cold cook items for manufacturing methamphetamine. Yet Ronald Baker, the renter of this home, was not arrested and properly charged on any of this, not to mention that he should have been viewed as a suspect in this murder case but was not.

Just minutes after Investigator Cundiff arrived on the scene, he was briefed by one of the deputies as to suspect Ronald Baker's version of the story. On the body cam, Investigator Cundiff and the deputy state, "This is pretty cut and dry." Keep in mind at this point, Investigator Cundiff had not interviewed any of the three residents of the trailer (a.k.a. suspects), had not searched anything, and had not seized any evidence, and yet he agreed that it was "pretty cut and dry" after less than ten minutes at the crime scene. This was later brought to the attention of the jury during the criminal trial through two of the officers with the body cameras, Investigator Cundiff and Bobby Jones, who later became sheriff. The jury had ample opportunity to view these body cams as they were played for them and submitted into evidence.

If the officers were not going to secure Ronald Baker in a police cruiser, then a police officer, not EMS, should have gotten Ronald Baker something else to keep him warm. But, as stated earlier, Ronald Baker should not have even been standing there in the first place. Ronald Baker had not been cleared by anyone at this point and was either a material witness *or* the shooter. He should have been separated from the crime scene and placed in the back of one of the many, many police cruisers one could see in these body cams. Ronald Baker then should have been taken to the police station, processed as a potential suspect in this case, and interrogated at the police station in a controlled environment. Ronald Baker's coat was laying just inches from the body but was not searched. It was part of the crime scene and should have been processed for evidence. None of this was done. The EMS person handed Ronald Baker his coat, and he was allowed to put it on and go to the shed unsupervised. As I watched this on the body cam, I was amazed at the very basic crime scene protocols that were not being followed.

On these body cams, people were shown just meandering around the potential crime scene area while providing no real assistance to the investigation. The cops, EMS, and the coroner waited almost an hour for Investigator Cody Cundiff to arrive. In this timeframe no one took charge of the scene and secured it. Finally a deputy took crime scene tape and surrounded the mobile home with it. He never asked the many bystanders to move from the crime scene. Way too much time passes when the body cams showed two officers beginning to clear the home for safety. Eventually one of these officers began to photograph the crime scene.

What is very visible, on both of the body cameras and in the photographs taken, are numerous methamphetamine pipes, syringes, and other drug paraphernalia. This was clearly a meth house and should have been treated as one with obvious possible connections to the shooting. This too was never done. Suspect Ronald Baker was never fully questioned about the drugs and paraphernalia at the crime scene and their possible relationship to the shooting. It was just glossed over, as if it did not matter. Whatever suspect Ronald Baker told the cops was taken at face value and without question. As I watched this unfold on the body cams and later in the recorded interviews of Ronald Baker, I was astonished at the lack of proper interview techniques and investigation. This murder scene was treated with all of the reverence of a barking dog call.

While the onlookers were standing around, two potential witnesses walked up to one of the officers who was wearing a body camera. On the body camera, you can hear a man asking, "Is this an active crime scene?" He also said to the officer, "My girlfriend and I live here, can we go and get our stuff out of the trailer?" The officer took down their names. It was a mother who lived across the road and her son who identified himself as a resident of the crime scene mobile home. The officer then asked for identification and allowed the man, James (name changed), to go to his mom's house and get his girlfriend's identification card. James told the officer that they had just come back from the store and did not know what was going on. James, his mother, and the girlfriend, Beth (name changed), were then allowed to simply disappear with no real investigation or interviews by the police—this, after James clearly tells the officer that he and Beth were residents of the mobile home (a.k.a. potential suspects and/or witnesses). Also noticed was the lack of concern from James as to who may have been hurt. What he is heard saying on the body cam—"Is this an active crime scene?"—should have raised an eyebrow of the officer as to why he would ask that. Why wasn't he asking "Who's hurt?" or "Is everyone okay?"

What should have happened after the officer learned that James and his girlfriend were residents of this crime scene was for them to have been separated and then interrogated/interviewed. Testing of their hands for gunshot residue, testing of their clothing for blood splatter, and DNA should have been done. At the minimum, the officer—not James the possible witness/suspect—should have gone to the house across the street himself and retrieved Beth's information. Or better yet, he should have placed both James and Beth in a police car to be taken to the police station for a videotaped interview and investigation.

Despite what James had told the officer, James and Beth were potentially material witnesses and quite possibly could have been the shooters. In the beginning of any crime scene, everyone is a suspect until properly ruled out by interviews and an objective investigation. James's story of them having been at the store should have been verified by one of the many police officers just standing around doing basically nothing. An officer should have gone to that particular store and ascertained if there was a video camera that supported his claim. Again, there were plenty of officers who could have been properly directed to do this but were not. Just because a resident of a crime scene says they were not present does not mean they are telling the truth. They should have been separated and taken to the station for questioning and further investigation. This never happened. Three possible witnesses or suspects to a murder were just allowed to walk off into the darkness. No evidence was seized from them and no GSR was taken from anyone in this case. What this witness did, in fact, state was that James and Beth were living at this residence where this murder took place. Yet they were never properly interviewed by the officers.

Almost an hour later, Investigator Cody Cundiff arrived on the scene. I noticed immediately that Investigator Cundiff was not wearing a body camera. The other officers' body cams clearly show that when Investigator Cundiff arrived, he was briefed by one of the deputies as to what Ronald Baker had told him. Ronald Baker had told the officer that he and his friend Clarence Roberts were just sitting on the couch watching TV when his son, Samuel Baker, pulled up and started an argument. Ronald Baker claimed he told his son to leave, but his son continued the argument. According to Ronald Baker, Clarence Roberts told Samuel he needed to respect his dad and just leave. Ronald Baker told police he went to his bedroom, sat down on the bed, and immediately heard three shots in rapid succession, bam, bam, bam. At that point he ran out of the bedroom and saw Clarence Roberts lying face down on the floor. He then heard a very loud car that he thought was his son's vehicle leaving the scene. He told officers that he did not see anything further; he only heard the shots.

The initial story told by Ronald Baker would change drastically over the course of the two interviews that night, a follow-up interview five days later, an interview three years later by the prosecutor the Friday just before the trial, and Ronald Baker's testimony to the jury. This changing of Ronald Baker's story was never questioned by Investigator Cundiff in any follow-up interviews. It was not until the Friday before the trial, three years later, that the prosecutor documented these glaring changes (a.k.a. potential lies) in a memo to the defense. These glaring changes were a point of focus at the trial and on cross-examination by defense attorney Jim Cox.

The body cams would then show Investigator Cundiff entering the mobile home with another officer. Investigator Cundiff did no real search of the residence; he stood adjacent to the victim's body, across from the other officer. The other officer was standing in the spot where the shooter would have probably shot from, just a couple of feet from the body. Investigator Cundiff asked the officer what he thought, and the officer is seen demonstrating on the body cam what he thought happened and from where the shooter shot. On the body cam, one can clearly see the officer putting his hands up to simulate a shooting position and then stating, "Probably right here." The officer was at the feet of the body. This was a very small area, and the body was lying between a small island and the refrigerator in the kitchen.

After I had fully investigated the evidence and personally visited and properly processed the crime scene, it was clear to me that the officer on the body camera was correct, and the shooter had been standing exactly where the officer said he was located at the time of the shooting. This would later be in direct contradiction to what Investigator Cundiff 's investigation (or lack thereof) would conclude. It would also be in direct contradiction to the story Ronald Baker had told, the same Ronald Baker who repeatedly stated he was in the bedroom and did not see the actual shooting.

If the shooter was in fact standing where the officer on the body cam and I had concluded was the correct spot, then logic would follow that the spent rounds would have ejected and landed between three to six feet at the shooter's right, in a three o'clock to five o'clock position from the shooter. From the evidence photographs, this would have placed the ejected rounds somewhere around the entry wall of the residence, near a stack of wood. On the body cam, it was obvious that Investigator Cundiff and at least two other officers thought the same thing because they were looking for the spent rounds at that very location, not outside on the ground. It is important to note that no spent rounds were located by the officers where the spent rounds should have been in this shooting, by or in the stack of wood located inside the house. The question is what happened to these spent rounds from the shooting, and who had the opportunity and motive to remove them? Could it have been Ronald Baker who had ample time? Remember, the devil is in the details.

Because the officers could not find spent rounds where they should have been, they assumed that spent rounds found outside of the trailer were the rounds fired the night of the murder. This would prove to be incorrect not only by Ronald Baker himself in interviews and on the witness stand during trial, but by Investigator Cundiff. Investigator Cundiff had written in his complaint that the spent rounds found outside the trailer were from a previous night when both Ronald Baker and his son Samuel Baker were shooting a 9mm handgun outside the trailer where the spent rounds were found.

Further, given the structure of the trailer, it is clear the shooter was not standing outside the trailer when the bullets were fired. In order for that to be possible, the bullets would have needed to make two right-angled turns to strike the victim at the points in which we know they did. This was later made clear by the defense to the jury during the criminal trial. However, the prosecutor told a different story of how the shooting happened, which to any trained professional was clearly wrong, thereby cramming a round peg into a square hole. The prosecution told the jury that the shooter was standing outside, where the spent rounds were found. Again, these are the same spent rounds that both Investigator Cundiff in his complaint and Ronald Baker clearly stated were rounds shot from a different night, not the night of the murder. If this crime scene had been properly processed with accurate measurements that were photographed, it should have been clear, even to a layperson, that the bullets could not make two right-angled turns in order to strike where this victim was obviously standing when he was hit.

Investigator Cundiff only spent minutes inside the crime scene residence the night of the shooting. He then asked where suspect Ronald Baker was located. Investigator Cundiff and Deputy Bobby Jones would then go to the small shed behind the home to interview Ronald Baker. It should be noted that no body cams for either Investigator Cundiff or Bobby Jones were produced by the prosecution. So, Investigator Cundiff and Deputy Jones, the lead investigators in this case, either did not wear body cams or the prosecution did not produce them. The question is why?

When asked this during the trial, the answers were absurd. One answer was that they didn't have to. Another was that there wasn't enough funding, and yet another was they didn't have enough storage for the information. At the trial, Deputy Jones (Sheriff Jones during the trial) stumbled over this answer with one excuse after another. Then he did what many bureaucrats do and gave a canned answer: "In all my years of experience we've always done it this way." This cliché is disconcerting, especially when it comes from an officer who has more than enough experience to know better. I am so tired of hearing this type of excuse from bureaucrats. News flash: just because you've been doing something for years does not mean you've been doing it right! No person, including this officer and his family members, would welcome such a cavalier attitude by a person who has the authority to charge them with murder.

When Sheriff Jones was further cross-examined during the trial about the three deputies turning off their body cams before leaving the crime scene and having gaps in time, Sheriff Jones had the same type of uninspiring answers. Sheriff Jones, Investigator Cundiff, and the three deputies with body cams admitted that they had no real policy or standard operating procedures for turning the cameras on and off. They used the excuse of storage of the information. With modern storage of information, including cloud-based and onsite storage, enormous amounts of information can be stored. This is shocking considering that it involves a murder where a jury will ultimately be asked to decide if a certain person committed the crime and set his punishment, which can be as severe as life imprisonment or even death. Again, it is extremely disturbing that incorrect use and/or failure to use body cams at a murder scene is not controlled in anyway by any regulations or standard operating procedures in the state of Kentucky. Once again, the lackadaisical approach the Kentucky general assembly has taken in ensuring the fair and uniform application of the law is staggering.

Investigator Cundiff and Deputy Bobby Jones did audio record their initial interview of Ronald Baker. While this is certainly better than no recording, it does not permit the listener to view Ronald Baker's demeanor. Oftentimes a person's demeanor can provide more information than their words, especially if you understand body language and have been trained to recognize cues showing deception. This first, very short interview took place outside, in the cold, at night. They make it clear from the outset that they believe Ronald Baker is not a suspect in this case, and the cops simply believe everything he has told them. They obtained Ronald Baker's basic information and asked him very few questions. Here is part of the transcript:

> **INVESTIGATOR CUNDIFF:** Okay, now that we got all that important stuff out of the way there, ah, I's going to say something, something took place here, what can you tell me about it?
>
> **RONALD BAKER:** Me and Clarence was just sitting there watching TV and stuff, and ah, we's waiting on Rhonda to come back in, and ah, and I, and I said, I told Clarence I don't think Rhonda was going to show up. And then, ah, this loud car pulled in the driveway, and it, and ah [inaudible], my son in the door, he was just here the other day and ah, pulled a gun on me.
>
> **CUNDIFF:** Um hum.
>
> **RB:** And ah, and I, he come in there and ah, I said Sam the best thing for you to do is just go on ahead and leave buddy, okay. Give me a few more days to get over this. And ah, Clarence said something to him, and he said you better listen to your dad. And then, and then he said it ain't none of his business is what we talk about. And I said, I said again, Sam, you just need to go, okay. You know. You just need to go.
>
> **CUNDIFF:** Yeah.
>
> **RB:** And uh, I said, well I'm gonna go and ah, I'm gonna go and ah, back here in the bedroom and, and go back to bed, make him think I'm in bed, you know what I'm saying, where you go on?

CUNDIFF: Um hum.

RB: Then when I got back there to the bedroom and I got in there and I turned around and I shut the door and I heard three shots [inaudible], and it was Clarence laying in the floor.

CUNDIFF: Okay.

RB: And the car was backing out of the driveway.

CUNDIFF: Who all was here, I know you said—

RB: It was me, him.

CUNDIFF: So I know you said it was you and Clarence watching TV—

RB: Yeah.

CUNDIFF: You was waiting for Rhonda to come back.

RB: Yeah, she didn't come back. She's well known for not coming back sometimes, you know what I'm saying.

CUNDIFF: Okay, so was there anybody else in the house when Sam got here?

RB: No.

CUNDIFF: No. Okay. And then, did Sam just automatically come on in the door or did he knock on the door? Or—

RB: No. [inaudible] come on in. I told him I didn't want him here.

CUNDIFF: Okay. And how long was you all in here talking or anything on those lines before you decided to walk back?

RB: About as long as it took me to say what I said, I walked to the bedroom, that's, that's the length of the time.

CUNDIFF: Okay.

RB: I don't know how long that was.

CUNDIFF: Okay. Ah, and then you said you heard three shots?

RB: [inaudible] laid Clarence, and I called 911.

CUNDIFF: Okay. And you said you heard Sam, you heard a loud car start up again and go to leave, right?

RB: Yeah.

CUNDIFF: Okay, and obviously Sam ain't out there now.

RB: No. Sam's one done it.

CUNDIFF: Okay. Okay.

RB: Yeah, Sam done it, I know damn good and well he did.

CUNDIFF: How old is he?

RB: Twenty-one, twenty-two. Somewhere's right in there.

CUNDIFF: Do you know his date of birth?

RB: December first is all I know and he's twenty-one, twenty-two years old.

CUNDIFF: Has he ever been in any trouble?

RB: Yes, yes, he has a felony record.

CUNDIFF: He does have a felony record?

RB: Yeah he has [inaudible].

[Partial cut of transcript for protection of innocent people.]

CUNDIFF: Okay. Uh, now you say it was ah, loud car, do you happen have any idea what kind of car?

RB: I have no idea. I know it was small and loud.

CUNDIFF: Okay.

RB: And it's a four cylinder.

DEPUTY JONES: Do you know what color it is?

RB: I couldn't tell, it was dark.

CUNDIFF: Okay. Um, now you said he came in here and he threatened you with a gun the other day.

RB: Yes, he did. I called law then too.

CUNDIFF: Okay, do you know what kind of gun it was that he—

RB: Nine millimeter. He shot the gun outside the door that night.

CUNDIFF: Ah huh.

RB: Right there. And I come out and I found the shell [inaudible] officer got here and I showed it to him.

CUNDIFF: Okay, you know what color it was or what brand or anything?

RB: All I know is it was nine millimeter shells, sir.

CUNDIFF: Okay. All right.

RB: You won't let me, I [inaudible], I ain't supposed to have a gun.

CUNDIFF: Did you see him with the gun today, whenever he came in the door?

RB: I didn't see the gun with him, no, I didn't see it in his hand. The last time he was here, he had it in his hand and apparently he had it with him, okay, he looked back out to the car.

CUNDIFF: Okay. Do you know where he normally keeps it if he's got it on him?

RB: [inaudible] belly.

CUNDIFF: [inaudible] belly?

RB: Yeah.

CUNDIFF: Okay. Okay. So whenever you heard, ah, Clarence telling him he needs to [inaudible] here and stuff like that.

RB: He said it was none of his business.

CUNDIFF: Okay.

RB: And uh . . .

CUNDIFF: Was there any threats made to Sam, or any—

RB: You don't know me, Sam said to him. You don't know who I am, you know.

CUNDIFF: Okay. Has Clarence got ah, a past too or what's the—

RB: No, Clarence was just ah, you need to go along cause I asked him to, you know, and that was it.

CUNDIFF: Okay. Can you can you think of anything?

JONES: Ah, who all lives in this house?

RB: Oh, well, right now a boy and a girl live here with me [yawns], excuse me.

JONES: Sure, no problem.

RB: It's ah, her son next door over here and his girlfriend.

JONES: [inaudible]

RB: Yeah, that one right here.

CUNDIFF: How long have they been staying here?

RB: Just one night.

JONES: Just one night?

RB: Just one night. Yeah, last night.

JONES: Okay.

RB: Now I take that back now, two nights now.

JONES: Two.

CUNDIFF: So they're a guest, they're not really, are you actually considering them living here or a guest?

RB: I give them a place to lay their head for awhile, yeah.

CUNDIFF: Okay.

RB: But ah, yeah.

CUNDIFF: Is there anybody else that actually lives here?

RB: No, just me.

JONES: Do you have a problem with us going through your house and looking at all that stuff?

RB: I don't care if you, yeah.

JONES: Okay.

RB: I[inaudible].

JONES: I mean, you're fine with us, I mean we've got, we've got a crime scene obviously, you know that.

RB: Why, yeah. [inaudible]

JONES: We got to look for shell casings and, and, and that kind of thing, and you don't have a problem with that.

RB: No.

CUNDIFF: The, the basis of what we're gonna be in here looking for is [inaudible].

RB: I know [inaudible] a gun [inaudible].

JONES: We're not ransacking your house.

RB: It's already been, that's what my boy did the other day when he was here, when he, he was here before I got here, and he had broke on in the house, and he [inaudible] bedroom, he was going through the drawers, yeah, the drawers was pulled out and everything, and I ain't put them back yet.

CUNDIFF: Okay. All right.

JONES: Well it's kind ah, cool tonight and, and ah, so we'll try to expedite this so we can get you back in the house and we can get you warm, will that be all right?

RB: It's gonna be fine, sir.

JONES: All right.

RB: But my phone's in there. I'd like to have it.

CUNDIFF: Do you know where it's at in there?

RB: Yeah, it's right there at the couch.

CUNDIFF: Right there on the couch?

RB: Right there on the couch.

There are many inconsistencies between this first interview and the second one, both of which were done on the night of the shooting, in the dark and cold.

Investigator Cundiff failed to treat Ronald Baker as a suspect. The first and second interviews were both rushed and no evidence was taken from this potential suspect. Remember, just because someone dials 911 does not mean they are not the killer. A seasoned, properly trained, proficient investigator should have taken Ronald Baker to the police station and made him wait for a proper interview. At the police station, Ronald Baker's hands should have been swiped for gunshot residue. This was not done. Investigator Cundiff should have taken Ronald Baker's clothes that he was wearing into evidence for possible blood splatter and powder residue. Ronald Baker should have been immediately searched upon arrival at the scene, yet he was never searched, as evidenced by the body cams. Ronald Baker's DNA should have been swabbed. This too was never done. Ronald Baker's cell phone should have been taken into custody to see who he was calling before, during, and after this shooting. This too was never done. Ronald Baker, as allegedly the only real witness in this case, should have been drug tested to ensure his ability to recall facts was not impaired on the night of the shooting. This also was not done. In fact, after the second very short interview, Ronald Baker was allowed to go back into the crime scene, the same crime scene where almost no real evidence was seized or attributed to Ronald Baker. Whatever evidence remained, or Ronald Baker had on his person, could now be easily destroyed, altered, or removed by him.

Had Investigator Cundiff taken his time, he would have found numerous inconsistencies in Ronald Baker's statements. Investigator Cundiff should have reviewed the 911 recording before interviewing Baker. This was not done even though the other officers had ample time to secure it prior to Investigator Cundiff's arrival. If he had reviewed it, a glaring inconsistency would have jumped out. In the interviews, Ronald Baker clearly tells Investigator Cundiff that he did not actually see the shooting. Ronald Baker told the 911 operator that Clarence was shot in the chest. Ronald Baker also tells the operator that Clarence is lying on his stomach. So how did Ronald Baker know that Clarence was shot in the chest if Clarence is lying on his stomach when Ronald Baker makes the 911 call? Remember, Ronald Baker has to roll Clarence over to check for breathing. Yet on the body cams, Ronald Baker clearly has no blood on him anywhere when the cops arrived. Investigator Cundiff should have questioned Ronald Baker on this issue and asked him if he had cleaned up, including changing clothes. Then Investigator Cundiff should have collected any clothing that Ronald Baker may have worn during the shooting. This was never done. Investigator Cundiff would never question Ronald Baker on how he would have known Clarence was shot in the chest, even though Ronald Baker claims that he did not see the shooting, and when he dialed 911, Clarence was on his stomach. The fact that this crucial line of questioning was never pursued as part of the investigation just baffles the mind.

At the crime scene, Investigator Cundiff left Ronald Baker unsupervised in a small shed and went back to the house. Minutes later he returned for the second interview. Here is some of the transcript of that second interview:

CUNDIFF: Mr. Baker, you doing all right out here?

RB: [inaudible]

CUNDIFF: What's that?

RB: I got a guy coming over, he's gonna let me sit in the truck with him.

CUNDIFF: Okay.

RB: He coming over.

CUNDIFF: Okay. Ah, let me ask you, the other day whenever your son was here and he fired some rounds off—

RB: Out here.

CUNDIFF: How many times did he shoot? Do you know?

RB: A couple of times.

CUNDIFF: Couple times, like couple times in two, or—

RB: Yeah [inaudible], yeah.

CUNDIFF: Just bam, bam?

RB: Yes.

CUNDIFF: Okay. Has he ever come over here and he shot in the back, right there any other time?

RB: Back there.

CUNDIFF: Way back there, though?

RB: No, right there, but he might of shot right here.

CUNDIFF: Okay. See, cause there's about three shell casings right here at the back door, and we've only found one inside.

RB: Well, where's you find it in there?

CUNDIFF: It was on the, on the bar.

RB: Okay, that's the one that I found out here the other day.

CUNDIFF: That's the one you found out here?

RB: Out here the other day. Yeah he [inaudible] happened right there, I think he shot him [inaudible] the door when he fired at him standing right there.

CUNDIFF: Okay.

RB: But he's fixing to push that strap on the door to keep him out—

[Cundiff keeps interrupting Baker]

CUNDIFF: Okay.

RB: I think that's what he was doing.

CUNDIFF: Okay. All right, that kind of sheds a bit of light on things then.

RB: Yeah.

CUNDIFF: All right, thank you.

RB: [inaudible] looks like he fell backwards into the chair, you know.

CUNDIFF: Yeah, that'd be my guess. Yeah. Okay. All right.

Again, if Investigator Cundiff had taken his time in these interviews and taken Ronald Baker to the nice, warm police station to videotape these interviews, perhaps he would have noticed the inconsistencies in his statements. This was not done. Another crucial thing I noticed in this interview that was later substantiated at trial is that the cops gave suspect Ronald Baker back his cell phone. Baker stated that, "I got a guy coming over, he's gonna let me sit in the truck with him." Cundiff just said okay. I was amazed that Investigator Cundiff and Deputy Jones simply returned a cell phone back to a suspect or material witness instead of seizing it to determine the activity on the night of the murder. Now we are left to wonder who Ronald Baker may have called before and after the shooting. This was yet another major FUBAR.

In this transcript, the officers allow Ronald Baker to become the crime scene investigator (CSI) for them, as he was allowed to point out where the rounds were and give impressions on what rounds were from which shooting. This too should never have been taken at face value. Investigator Cundiff, in his later sketches of the crime scene, simply duplicated what suspect Ronald Baker told him. There was no further investigation other than CSI Ronald Baker's rendition of the sequence of events. The sequence of events should have been verified independently of the rendition by Ronald Baker. Talented investigators have an innate curiosity with crime scenes. In this instance, Investigator Cundiff seems to have allowed his complacency with Ronald Baker to supplant his curiosity of the crime scene. The question remains: Did this happen because he was under a cloud with the investigation into the missing evidence/currency?

Ronald Baker in the first interview clearly stated that he never saw the shooting. Yet in the second interview, Ronald Baker is providing a detailed description of where the victim was standing and what he was doing at the moment he was shot:

> **RB:** Out here the other day. *Yeah he [inaudible] happened right there, I think he shot him [inaudible] the door when he fired at him standing right there.*
>
> **CUNDIFF:** Okay.
>
> **RB:** *But he's fixing to push that strap on the door to keep him out—*
>
> **[Cundiff keeps interrupting Baker]**
>
> **CUNDIFF:** Okay.
>
> **RB:** I think that's what he was doing.

Doing an interview in a dark, cold shed in a rushed fashion also caused Investigator Cundiff to completely miss the fact that Ronald Baker had no blood on his clothes. At trial we did a demonstration in front of Ronald Baker on the stand. Ronald Baker confirmed to the jury the manner in which we demonstrated turning the body over was, in fact, how he had turned the body over as well. The point was to demonstrate to the jury that it was virtually impossible for Ronald Baker to have turned over the body without getting at least some blood on his hands, arms, and clothing. The victim was a pretty big guy and would have been difficult to turn over. Yet we posted still shots from the body cameras for the jury that clearly showed Ronald Baker had no blood on him when the officers arrived. Did he change clothes and get cleaned up? We will never know definitively, nor will we know what trace evidence the clothes potentially contained. We do know the clothes of Ronald Baker were never collected and any evidence is irretrievably lost.

Under cross-examination, when asked if he changed his clothes, Ronald Baker denied it and said there probably was blood on him. Again, because the investigators failed to treat Ronald Baker as a suspect and seize his clothes and shoes and swab his hands and arms on the night of the shooting, we will never know. This should have been done not only to see if he had changed clothes and washed up, but also to determine if there was any type of blood splatter pattern on Ronald Baker and his clothes. If analyzed correctly, blood splatter can be invaluable in determining a person's proximity to a victim at the time an injury is inflicted. Since Ronald Baker stated that he was not present when the shots were fired, neither he nor his clothes should have contained any blood splatter. The blood that should have been on Ronald Baker, but was not, would be the blood from a contact transfer when he turned the victim over.

Ronald Baker's trailer should have been more thoroughly searched for the clothing from which Ronald Baker had likely changed. The fact that this too was never done should be most disturbing to all who read this. This is crime scene investigation 101. Either you choose to believe that these cops were never properly trained in even the most basic steps on how to properly process a crime scene, *or* they were complacent in their jobs and are ignoring their training.

When interviews are rushed or conducted improperly, important evidence like this will be missed. After these two short interviews and almost no searching or seizing of anything at the crime scene, Ronald Baker, with cell phone in hand having never been properly searched, was allowed to simply go back into the crime scene to do anything he wanted with any potential evidence that was not recovered. This is probably why the cops and prosecutor were so reluctant to produce those body cams. They truly expose the lack of an investigation that night. Investigator Cundiff, the lead investigator in this case, spent less than two hours at this crime scene. When he left, so did all of the other police officers, who for many hours were just standing around idly except for taking photos and listening to Ronald Baker's unchallenged version of the facts.

Had someone taken over this crime scene in a timely manner, these extra officers could have been properly interviewing witnesses and transporting them to the police station for proper interrogations and seizing of evidence from their bodies and clothing. Instead, what we clearly see from the body cams are officers just standing around with their hands in their pockets, waiting for orders, as they trample all over the crime scene. They did take many photos of the crime scene but no real, thorough search for weapons, spent rounds, or any type of evidence is shown on these body cams.

The body of the victim, Clarence Roberts, was never searched at the scene. It was later searched at the medical examiner's office, where they found a quantity of methamphetamine under a tennis sweatband on the victim's wrist. This should have been found by the investigators at the crime scene. The victim was an elderly man, who was in a soft cast and could barely walk much less play tennis. Yet investigators never questioned why he had a tennis type of sweatband on his wrist or examined it. This could have been easily done without disturbing the body. During the trial, the officer's excuse was that the coroners did not want the officer moving the body. Coroners do not dictate how officers conduct a murder investigation. To be clear, crime scenes should be controlled by investigating officers, not third parties such as a coroner, witnesses, family members, or others.

Nowhere on the body cams do we see anyone, including the lead investigator, doing an actual search. No one looks under the couches or cushions. No one does any type of real search for a weapon at the crime scene. The investigator simply takes Ronald Baker's word that his son was the shooter and the weapon left the crime scene with him. Again, at no time does anyone even search Ronald Baker who, in any real investigation, would most certainly be a suspect until he was properly ruled out. None of this was ever done.

Later that night Investigator Cundiff and then–Deputy Jones conducted an interview of Samuel Baker. Samuel did not talk to them except to say, "I have the right to remain silent," and that's what he did. No attempts were made by the investigators to obtain gunshot residue from Sam's hands. No attempts were made to obtain gunshot residue from the steering wheel of the vehicle Samuel Baker was driving when he was arrested. If the excuse for not examining Sam's hands was because he was wet and it was raining, then it did not apply to his steering wheel since it was not wet. Under the theory of transference, had Sam been the shooter and then immediately entered his vehicle and fled the scene, then there was a good chance he would have transferred the gunshot residue from his hands to the steering wheel and other areas of his vehicle. If no gunshot residue was found on Sam and gunshot residue was perhaps found on either Ronald Baker or the other residents, this would have bolstered Samuel Baker's not guilty claim. This too was not done by the investigators.

Almost three years later, the prosecutor in this case sent Samuel Baker's phone, clothing, and shoes to the lab for processing. None of this had been done by the investigators in the prior three years. Sam Baker's clothing came back with no evidence that he was ever at the scene on the night of the shooting. Further, there were no cell phone pings showing that Sam Baker was even in Pulaski County on the night of the shooting. This too was made clear to the jury.

On the night of the crime Ronald Baker was allowed to go back into the crime scene and take control, yet his phone and body were never searched. Gunshot residue samples were never completed on Ronald Baker, and his clothing was not taken into evidence for examination. No fingerprints were ever dusted by anyone at the crime scene. No attempts were made to obtain footprints or tire prints at the crime scene. No DNA was ever taken from Ronald Baker or the other two residents for comparisons. No actual measurements of the crime scene were ever documented. Other than the word of a previously convicted drug dealer, who was admittedly on drugs on the night of the shooting, there was no physical evidence showing that Sam Baker was even at that crime scene on the night of the shooting.

By doing these simple investigative tasks, the investigators could have either excluded Ronald Baker as a suspect or arrested him. They did not. This created a conundrum when Sam Baker later said that he did not commit the crime when he pleaded not guilty. The question then became the following: Was Sam Baker actually guilty and attempting to avoid accountability, or was he innocent and attempting to protect his aging father? Investigator Cundiff and then–Deputy Jones had no idea for sure what Sam was going to say that night. They just assumed that Ronald Baker was telling the truth. They just assumed they could get Sam Baker to confess to them or at least make incriminating statements. But that is not what happened.

Investigations are about ensuring the innocent are not wrongly accused just as much as they are about ensuring the guilty do not escape accountability. By the time the cops should have realized that their handling of the crime scene, suspects, and witnesses was a FUBAR of gigantic proportions, it was too late. You only get one chance at a crime scene investigation, and Ronald Baker was allowed back inside with his cell phone in hand to do as he wished. Now any evidence pointing to anyone else besides Sam Baker was most certainly compromised when they turned the crime scene back over to suspect Ronald Baker. Thus, as we would later learn after forensics, without Ronald Baker's testimony, the cops had no real physical evidence that Sam Baker was even at the crime scene the night of the murder. Ronald Baker's word was the only thing linking Sam to the crime scene. The lack of properly ruling out Ronald Baker or the other two residents as suspects by accurately searching and processing evidence, on them and in the mobile home, leaves any future judge and jury in the unenviable position of having to make crucial decisions without the benefit of having access to fundamental evidence. In fact, there was more physical evidence linking Ronald Baker to the crime scene than Sam. If that is not bad enough, we would later learn that Ronald Baker is a previously convicted drug dealer who served six years for illegally selling pills. Investigator Cundiff knew this and still trusted Ronald Baker completely.

As a result, during the trial the prosecution could present no physical evidence that Sam Baker was at the crime scene on the night of the shooting—other than the words of a convicted drug dealer. They presented spent rounds outside the trailer as the spent rounds from the murder. They did this despite the fact that Ronald Baker's testimony at trial, his three interviews, and Investigator Cundiff's very own complaint were in direct opposition to this theory.

Sam Baker's location at the time of his arrest was in a different county, Casey County, Kentucky. He was pulled over on an unrelated incident. The gun seized in Casey County was found in a rain-soaked wooded area. Photographs of this Casey County gun at the seizure location showed the gun lying wet on the ground. This would make accurate recovery of DNA evidence difficult if not impossible. Further, the Casey County gun would remain in the Pulaski County Sheriff's Office evidence room for months before it was submitted to the Frankfort lab for testing. The Casey County gun sat in the same evidence room during the same time that the lead investigator on this case and the evidence room itself were under investigation for missing evidence/currency. (Yeah, no problems here.) This understandably and naturally generated a cloud of suspicion and uncertainty on all of the evidence by those it would be used against.

At trial Ronald Baker knew his DNA would most likely be on the Casey County gun. He testified that several nights before the murder, he had handled the Casey County gun in order to teach Sam Baker to disassemble and reassemble it. First, Ronald Baker had left this information out of all three of his previous interviews. Second, there was in fact two other people's DNA on the Casey County gun. Ronald Baker's DNA was never taken for comparison by the police, so it was unclear if his DNA was on the Casey County gun. However, the DNA expert testified that there was, in fact, the DNA of two other people on the Casey County gun but not Sam Baker. Consequently, neither the ballistics expert nor the DNA expert could exclude Ronald Baker as the shooter. This too was made clear to the jury.

On March 23, 2021, Investigator Cundiff returned to the crime scene to conduct the third follow-up interview of Ronald Baker—five days after the shooting. The recording of this interview once again demonstrated numerous inconsistencies between Ronald Baker's 911 call, the first interview, the second interview, and this third interview. In this third recorded interview, Investigator Cundiff repeatedly refers to Ronald Baker as "buddy." Ronald Baker is allowed, once again, to point out more evidence, this time in a paper towel holder. Ronald Baker told Investigator Cundiff that there was a bullet lodged in a wall from the shooting behind the paper towel holder. This seemed strange given that Ronald Baker claimed, as stated in his previous interviews and on the 911 tape, he did not witness the shooting but then stated he knew there was a bullet from that night lodged in the wall behind a paper towel roll. Did Ronald Baker know about this round on the night of the shooting? Was this just another distraction to divert Investigator Cundiff from the real interrogation? These would have been good questions for Investigator Cundiff to have asked, but instead he allowed Ronald Baker to once again control the narrative and the crime scene evidence, which never should have happened.

Further, why did Ronald Baker not point this paper towel holder evidence out to Investigator Cundiff on the night of the shooting, and why did the search (or lack thereof) of the crime scene not find it? Why did Investigator Cundiff not question him about this new evidence? Why did Investigator Cundiff not measure the trajectory of this newly found round and photograph it since the location of the shooter was unclear?

What happened later in this third interview was nothing short of astonishing. When Investigator Cundiff could not dig the paper towel round out of the wall, he simply instructed Ronald Baker to try dig it out later and collect it as evidence. Investigator Cundiff stated, "If you can get it out, just give me a call." It is never appropriate to allow a potential suspect or witness to gather evidence, especially in a murder case. Here again, Investigator Cundiff's unmitigated trust in a potential suspect is a manifestation of someone not committed to his work. When Investigator Cundiff was asked about this at trial, he had no clear or good answers for allowing a layperson to collect important evidence. To be honest, Investigator Cundiff looked unprofessional on the stand and admitted that he was no longer an investigator/detective. He just referred to himself as "Sergeant Cundiff." To me this was very telling. This department and the prosecutor had spent an inordinate amount of time and effort trying to pretend that Investigator Cundiff was not the investigator on this case. This began almost immediately after Investigator Cundiff flunked the polygraph and continued right up through the trial. The prosecutor didn't even use Investigator Cundiff to testify at the grand jury hearing.

In the third interview with Ronald Baker, Investigator Cundiff spent considerable time trying to get that round out of the paper towel holder and wall. Yet on the evening of the actual shooting, Investigator Cundiff spent less than two hours on the entire investigation, which included interviews, searching, and processing of evidence at the actual crime scene.

In his three interviews, two on the night of the shooting and one five days later, Ronald Baker clearly changes his story of where Sam Baker was standing when he allegedly shot the victim. At first, Ronald Baker indicated that Sam Baker must have been standing outside because of where he found the spent rounds in this investigation. Then he indicated that Sam must have been inside because of the round in the wall, through the paper towel roll. Yet in his first statements, he said he did not see any of the shooting. He claimed he was in his bedroom with the door closed. Either Investigator Cundiff did not recognize these inconsistencies or he chose to overlook them because they did not conform to his preconceived notions of what happened. He never questioned Ronald Baker on these inconsistencies.

In his third interview, Ronald Baker told Investigator Cundiff that he served six years in prison for possession and for sale of illegal narcotics, and Investigator Cundiff acknowledged he knew about that case and recognized Ronald Baker from it. So Investigator Cundiff knew Ronald Baker was a drug dealer, and yet he naively trusted Ronald Baker's explanations about the crime scene and shooting. Astonishingly, the round in the wall behind the paper towel roll was never retrieved from the wall, subjected to testing and comparison, and/or never submitted as evidence. It is inconceivable that a bullet that could possibly be used to include or exclude a specific gun to a murder was not retrieved and tested. This too was made clear to the jury during the trial.

Also in his third interview, Investigator Cundiff informed Ronald Baker that he was going across the road to interview the two people, James and Beth, who were living with Ronald Baker at the time of the shooting. We have no evidence this interview ever happened. No recordings or reports were ever submitted to the defense. Moreover, the proper time to have questioned these two potential witnesses/suspects was on the night of the shooting when one of them actually approached a deputy and informed him that he lived there and wanted to get some of his belongings. This conversation was on a deputy's body cam from the night of the shooting. Yet there is no evidence that these all-important interviews were ever conducted by investigators from the Pulaski County Sheriff's Office. At the trial, when Investigator Cundiff was questioned about this, he told the jury that he did in fact interview these witnesses/suspects across the street but had failed to record those interviews. When asked why, he said his recorder had run out of batteries and he did not have any more with him. I found this to be one of the biggest BS stories I've ever heard, consistent with "the dog ate my homework." This is precisely why Investigator Cundiff should have taken all of the witnesses/suspects down to the station and properly conducted a videotaped interview/ interrogation of them all. At the very least, he could have used a body camera to memorialize the interviews.

On the Friday before the actual trial, over three years after the shooting and at precisely four p.m., our defense team received a statement of interview of Ronald Baker from the prosecutor David Dalton. In this interview, and later on the stand, Ronald Baker again changed his story. He clearly stated, for the first time in over three years, that on the night of the murder, both he and the victim were doing meth—a fact that made him an unreliable witness to events on the night of the shooting. He also stated for the first time that he had previously handled the Casey County gun (a.k.a. alleged murder weapon) and that the rounds found outside his trailer were from several nights before the actual murder. Remember, these were the only spent rounds that the ballistics expert was using to link Sam Baker to the shooting. If these rounds were shot on a previous night, as stated by Ronald Baker under oath during the trial and written in Investigator Cundiff 's report, then there was absolutely no physical evidence linking Sam Baker to the murder scene on the night of the murder. The fact that the prosecutor produced this in a document on a Friday evening before the trial was nothing short of astonishing. My guess was he was hoping that defense counsel Jim Cox would request a postponement, which was not granted.

The fact that Ronald Baker was high from drugs the night of the murder made him an obviously unreliable witness. Investigator Cundiff or then–Deputy Jones could have easily made this determination from observation and a drug test on the night of the shooting. This is why Ronald Baker should have been taken to the station, properly processed, and drug tested! This was not done. On the witness stand during the trial, Ronald Baker admitted to being on drugs that night and "partying" with the victim. During the trial and under cross-examination, attorney

Jim Cox asked Ronald Baker where he got the drugs he had used on the day of the murder. Ronald Baker's answer was, "The getting place." Jim pressured Ronald Baker into divulging his drug dealer's name, but he refused. Finally, Judge Whitaker told Ronald Baker to reveal the name. Ronald Baker's demeanor drastically changed from the victim the prosecutor was portraying him to be. He revealed himself to be the angry, deceitful drug dealer he really was. After a few moments of just sitting there angry in front of the jury, Ronald Baker gave what appeared to be a fictitious name, which would never be verified by law enforcement. This thoroughly revealed that this addict drug dealer would deceive even a court and jury to protect his dealer and himself, all while freely sacrificing his son Sam. This too was somehow lost on the jury even though it was clearly demonstrated during the trial.

Approximately one week after the shooting, then–Deputy Bobby Jones testified before the grand jury on this case. At no time during this testimony did Jones ever disclose to the grand jury that the lead investigator, Cody Cundiff, was under investigation for missing currency/evidence from the evidence room. At no time was there any reference to the fact that the evidence room was under state investigation for missing evidence/currency. At no time did Deputy Jones ever state that he was not the lead investigator or why Investigator Cundiff was not giving testimony before the grand jury on this case. Omitting crucial facts that leave a grand jury unaware of important details could be viewed as deceitful. Apparently the prosecutor knew about the scandal of the missing evidence/currency and did not want Investigator Cundiff anywhere near his case, thus placing Deputy Jones on the stand.

In later evidence hearings prior to trial, only Bobby Jones, now Sheriff Jones, would be available to answer attorney Jim Cox's questions. Further, the grand jury never knew Ronald Baker was a convicted felon for drug dealing and served six years; they never knew Ronald Baker was doing meth with the victim the night of the murder. The grand jury also never knew the bullet in the body was not a match to the Casey

County gun. The grand jury also never knew the spent rounds being presented as the murder rounds were not from the night of the shooting (as previously documented in Investigator Cundiff's report). The grand jury also never heard that there was absolutely no physical evidence (no gunshot residue, no fingerprints, no DNA, no blood splatter evidence, no tire prints, no footprints, and no cell phone pings) directly linking Sam Baker to the crime scene on the night of the murder. They only heard what the prosecutor wanted them to hear, and that Sam Baker tried to run when he was pulled over in another county. Had the grand jury known any of these other material facts, perhaps they would have questioned this indictment. Moreover, all of this was in fact relayed to the jury during the murder trial.

The evidence property report provided by the prosecutor of the evidence in this murder case was dated April 1, 2021. It listed seventeen items but no one on the form signed this evidence into the evidence locker. There was no indication of who received this evidence into the evidence room, no log, and no real chain of custody. Keep in mind that this occurred during the time frame that Investigator Cundiff was a suspect in the missing evidence/currency taken from the Pulaski County Sheriff's Office evidence room. According to the KSP investigator's report, the master key and log had disappeared as well.

On the KSP's request for examination form in this murder case, there was again no signature from the officer who had submitted this evidence. Further, this form had the wrong offense date. Just days before the trial, the form mysteriously appeared with Investigator Cundiff's signature. This also revealed that Investigator Cundiff, not any other deputy, was in fact the lead investigator on this case and the prosecution was struggling to hide this fact.

The ballistics evidence in this murder case was not submitted to the KSP lab until May 6, 2021—just under two months after the murder. The second set of ballistics evidence was not submitted until June 15, 2021. Why the delay? Why were these submissions separated? Furthermore, at this point Investigator Cundiff knew the spent rounds found outside the trailer were not from the night of the shooting. This was made clear by Ronald Baker and memorialized in Investigator Cundiff's complaint. Clearly this was inappropriate and served as an amateurish attempt to fit a square peg in a round hole.

On August 31, 2021, five months after the shooting, an unsigned DNA sample card request was sent in with Investigator Cundiff's name typed on the memo, requesting the victim's DNA. The question is, why wait five months after a shooting for this?

On June 6, 2021, the request for evidence examination form was finally signed for by the central lab, yet the submission was dated April 28, 2021. Where was this evidence from March 18to June 6? Was it in the back of Investigator Cundiff's car? Because of the shenanigans in the Pulaski County sheriff's evidence room, there is no definite proof of where this or any of the evidence was actually located at any particular time. There was no real documented chain of custody. Whoever had the missing master key had carte blanche access to the evidence room, access to the evidence computer system, and could make changes at will. This is precisely why evidence room procedures and oversight are so important, but virtually absent from this particular evidence room.

On June 15, 2021, the Frankfort lab produced a document indicating that it had received a "Hi-Point 9mm Luger; one live 9mm Luger cartridge; one magazine and two live 9mm luger cartridges." Again, this shooting was just under three months prior, and they were only now receiving this all-important evidence. The location of this evidence for the past three months is unclear. After having been subjected to the unsecure evidence room, any DNA or other evidence was simply not trustworthy. This is especially true for DNA evidence potentially on a firearm, which must be handled with the utmost care and a strict adherence to the proper chain of custody procedures. This was clearly not done in this case.

There is an unsigned memo from Investigator Cundiff dated August 12, 2021, documenting that he had sent a DNA sample card of the victim to the KSP lab in Frankfort requesting a comparison. This occurred almost five months after the shooting. Why this delay and why didn't Investigator Cundiff sign these documents? Perhaps because the prosecutor and/or sheriff wanted to distance Investigator Cundiff from this murder investigation?

On December 2, 2021, a search warrant was executed on Investigator Cundiff's accounts by KSP Detective Michael Keeton, in reference to the missing currency/evidence from the Pulaski County Sheriff's Office evidence room. While nothing really ever came of this, it is certain that being under investigation and getting served with search warrants would have had an impact on Investigator Cundiff's ability to process a murder investigation properly. Even with this much mounting pressure, Investigator Cundiff was left on this murder case to process crucial evidence.

On January 5, 2022, the DNA analysis was completed on a cloth from the 9mm seized in Casey County from the alleged shooter, Sam Baker. This analysis, which was almost a year after the shooting, demonstrated a "mixture of three people" in this case. As mentioned, a comparison between this 9mm and DNA could not be made with the other possible shooter, Ronald Baker, because the investigators failed to obtain DNA samples or any other evidence (clothing, shoes) from Ronald Baker and the other residents of the home. Consequently, their DNA was not submitted to the lab. This was, once again, a crucial mistake in basic crime scene investigation. The investigator in this case did nothing to rule out suspect Ronald Baker or the other two residents as the potential shooters. The cops simply believed what an obvious suspect told them and allowed Ronald Baker to become their CSI. This should never have happened. Even if Ronald Baker was not the shooter, this type of casual and unsystematic work would allow any half-witted defense attorney, much less a seasoned expert like Jim Cox, to place reasonable doubt in a jury's mind as to who really was the shooter. This burdened the jury with two choices: adopt the cops' untested assumptions or just guess at the shooter's identity.

On March 17, 2022, one year after the shooting, there was a letter from Jon Williams to Major Hancock. In a pertinent part, it stated, "movement of missing items to new location . . . I have moved all the items that were found to be missing when I completed the inventory in 2019–2020 to this location." This leaves us wondering, what items were found? What items were missing? Were items missing then found and moved regarding this murder case? This was never detailed in either KSP Detective Keeton's report or any other document.

On June 4, 2022, again over one year after missing currency/evidence and the shooting, KSP Detective Keeton filed for a search warrant for records in the missing money case. There is nothing like waiting over a year to finally do some investigation. This is indicative of an evidence room in chaos and an extremely slow and botched investigation into it. This also leaves us wondering, was KSP Detective Keeton's investigation slow-walked because the sheriff at the time of the missing currency/evidence was a former KSP commander? Or did the fact that Deputy Robert "Bobby" Jones was running for sheriff at the time have a bearing on this investigation?

On June 28, 2022, the Kentucky Association of Counties (KACo) issued a check for reimbursement to the Pulaski County Sheriff's Office for $25,447, minus a $250 deductible. This was paid despite the huge cloud hanging over this evidence room. This is reminiscent of the adage, "When it is the taxpayers' money, it's nobody's money."

Ironically, on August 17, 2022 (almost a year and a half after the Faubush-Norfleet shooting), the missing master key to the evidence room was found in the trunk of a Pulaski County Sheriff's Office motor pool vehicle. No one knows, or at least is telling, how this important key got into the trunk of a vehicle accessible by a multitude of people. This key allowed access to this evidence room and evidence in this all-important murder case to anyone willing to use it. Evidence could have been altered, removed, or supplemented, including changing dates. Who knows what happened while no one was watching.

On August 22, 2022, while Investigator Cundiff was the lead investigator on this case and after having flunked a polygraph regarding the missing evidence/currency, Investigator Cundiff was removed as the evidence custodian yet allowed to remain on this murder case and process evidence.

On August 23, 2022, Sheriff Speck gave an interview regarding the missing $25,000 from his evidence room. In this interview he assured the public that "there was no other items unaccounted for." This was simply not true. There were memos dating back from 2015 that clearly revealed numerous items of evidence were missing. These memos were addressed to Sheriff Speck. At this point, there was the appearance that the sheriff's office was obfuscating the fact that there was missing evidence.

On October 6, 2022 (over a year and a half after the Faubush-Norfleet shooting), there was a memo from the Frankfort lab stating that analysis had started. On October 11, 2022, the ballistics report from Frankfort was issued. So it only took six days to conduct analysis on this firearm, but it sat at the lab for over a year and a half? Again, one would think this was a low-level misdemeanor case, given the manner in which it was treated at every step of the investigation, rather than a murder case.

On November 3, 2022, the local commonwealth attorney submitted a letter to KSP Detective Keeton regarding the evidence room and the missing evidence/currency. Part of the letter states that "the time frame for the possible theft is between 2015 and 2021 . . . Lack of appropriate oversight and evidence review also makes this case very problematic for prosecution." So this evidence room is pilfered but no one is fired or goes to jail, and yet the evidence from this compromised evidence room is used to send someone to prison for life. While this is per se incredible, the most disturbing facet of this problem is that no one in Kentucky is developing any solutions to address it.

On June 10, 2023, attorney Jim Cox and I interviewed and video-taped Jessica A. Copeland. She is the forensic scientist specialist who conducted forensics on the firearm and ballistics in this murder case. It is important to note that prior to this interview, courts, including the Kentucky Supreme Court, have made several rulings in cases involving investigators using shell casings found at the crime scene to match to a firearm seized from another location and linked to a particular suspect. (See references section at the end of the book for more information.)

Kentucky's highest appellate court stated the following: "If you have the gun and both rounds they can testify to reasonable degree of certainty that the rounds are consistent with each other, but can not say it is beyond a shadow of doubt that both rounds were fired from the same gun." This is exactly what the prosecution in this Faubush-Norfleet murder case was trying to do. The prosecutor and his ballistics expert were trying to make the unsubstantiated and inappropriate leap that the spent rounds found outside the trailer were in fact the spent rounds used in the murder. This was despite the fact that not only did Investigator Cundiff clearly state otherwise in his complaint but also Ronald Baker gave opposing testimony to this very thing at trial. Ronald Baker unmistakably testified at trial that the spent rounds found in the yard were generated from a previous night when he and Sam Baker were shooting—round peg, square hole. Yet the ballistics expert was trying to convince the jury that these spent rounds were from the night of the shooting.

On the ballistics report, it clearly stated that the round from the victim's body could not be matched to the Casey County gun, the alleged murder weapon. Yet the ballistics expert testified that "it may or may not be a match; that she couldn't rule it out." The reason the Kentucky Supreme Court prohibits testimony such as this is to prevent ostensible experts from overreaching in their conclusions. The round from the body could have also been from ten thousand other 9mm handguns, one of the most common handguns sold in the United States and Kentucky, and/or from one of the other previous shootings documented in 911 reports that had happened at this location. This was extremely misleading by the ballistics expert and clearly misstated the facts. Defense attorney Jim Cox countered her testimony during cross-examination and again in his closing argument with the fact that she could not match this round from the body to the alleged murder weapon found in Casey County. This was made clear to the jury during this trial.

The examiners in these prior Kentucky Supreme Court cases testified at trial that the rounds found at the crime scene had come from the same guns linked to the suspects' guns and the suspects were convicted. The problem with the methodology used by these ostensible experts is that numerous published studies in peer review journals show that this science is highly flawed when firearms and tool mark examiners apply it. Yet it is presented to jurors as precise and exact.

Also in numerous prior appellate rulings, in Kentucky and elsewhere, examiners are instructed to follow scientific protocol that requires the following: the examination must be verifiable and reproducible (in other words, not just one round shot from suspect weapon); must have a second, independent, qualified examiner from the lab review the work or conclusions in accordance with the generally accepted standard in the field; and the lab must have outside peer review. These protocols are standard scientific methods accepted by the American Society of Crime Laboratory Directors, the FBI, and the President's Council of Advisors on Science and Technology (PCAST).

In our interview with Copeland, which we videotaped, she clearly admits that she and her fellow ballistics experts at the Frankfort lab follow none of these standard protocols recognized by the courts. My jaw literally dropped when she stated, "We have our own protocols" when asked what protocols she followed. She stated that there were no outside peer reviews, and her examination was not repeated by a separate examiner to ensure the results could, in fact, be repeated. This is a clear violation of standard scientific protocol that most agencies are required to follow. She stated that the only person reviewing her work was her supervisor at the Frankfort lab. Even if all the protocols are followed, most courts have ruled an expert opining that a particular firearm matches recovered projectiles or cartridge casings is limited to a "reasonable degree of ballistic certainty." They are not allowed to testify and/or insinuate they have an exact match.

Further, her report stated that the spent cartridges found by suspect Ronald Baker at the crime scene were identified as "having been fired in item 1," the 9mm Luger found in Casey County. She also stated that, *"Item 8 (One bullet) could neither be identified as having been fired from item 1, due to insufficient correspondence of individual characteristics."* In other words, in her report she could not truthfully state that this particular 9mm Luger was the weapon that fired the shots that killed the victim in this case. She could also not truthfully testify that the spent rounds found at the crime scene were an exact match to the round fired from the weapon found that night, in the rain, in the woods in Casey County, allegedly belonging to suspect Sam Baker. Yet during the trial, these were precisely her new and improved conclusions.

Moreover, there were several rounds seized at the crime scene only after suspect Ronald Baker and an EMT pointed them out to the investigators. Ronald Baker also told them that prior to this shooting, other people had been on his property shooting with other 9mm handguns, in addition to Ronald Baker and Sam Baker. This was later verified in prior police reports and 911 call logs. Therefore, Copeland could not truthfully testify that she could completely, 100 percent exclude any and all other 9mm handguns that may have fired spent rounds found by suspect Ronald Baker and used by the prosecution in this case. This was also clearly documented in Investigator Cundiff's complaint filed in this case. During trial, this great gaping hole in the prosecutor's case was also repeatedly brought to the attention of the jury by attorney Jim Cox.

In our interview with Copeland, she stated that when she fired the Casey County 9mm Luger allegedly involved in this shooting, she noticed it was very difficult to fire and the magazine would not stay in the pistol without assistance. She stated that she had to physically hold the magazine and push up on it in order to get the gun to fire. Amazingly enough, none of this was documented in her initial report. However, this was suspiciously explained and magically cured in a supplemental report given to the defense just three days before the trial and three years after the shooting. I found this highly suspicious. In this new ballistics report, again just three days before trial, she documented that the magazine would not stay in the pistol without assistance and this made it difficult to fire. This leaves one to wonder: Just how accurate could an inexperienced shooter be with a firearm that was difficult to shoot, even for a ballistics expert, if the prosecution's theory of where the shooter was standing, outside the mobile home and shooting upward at angles that only a magic bullet could make, were true?

In an email dated June 25, 2021, from KSP lab technician Sara Lamb to Investigator Cundiff, she seems confused about the evidence that Investigator Cundiff submitted. She submitted a plethora of questions, including the following: "Could you provide more information about the gun? The KSP26 list a Hi-Point 9mm was found in the area. What is its association? Why was the cloth submitted? Does the knife need to be analyzed for blood? Is it known if the suspect was bleeding at the time of the incident? Are you able to obtain any blood or buccal standard from the victim?"

I found this amazing, and not in a good way. Apparently when Investigator Cundiff submitted this all-important evidence to the lab, he did not indicate on the KSP forms what he wanted done with this evidence. It is a major mistake for an investigating officer to fail to provide proper instructions to the lab on what test he wanted conducted on the evidence. The lab technicians need this information so they can properly organize the sequence of the tests, among other things. For example, if you want DNA from a firearm, you must inform the lab of this so that they send it to the DNA lab before it is sent to ballistics. If the firearm is sent to ballistics or anywhere else first, the examiners and everyone else handling the firearm will adulterate the DNA. As indicated by other emails, the 9mm went to ballistics first and then to the lab for DNA testing. This was a major mistake by Investigator Cundiff, who gave no instructions to the lab on this evidence. Perhaps being under investigation himself regarding the evidence room had Investigator Cundiff distracted from this investigation.

On July 23, 2021, Investigator Cundiff responded to the examiner's request regarding the DNA sample. Investigator Cundiff belatedly obtained a DNA comparison for the victim from the Louisville medical examiner's office—four months after the shooting.

In an email from the medical examiner dated August 12, 2021, Investigator Cundiff had still not submitted the proper paperwork or letter to the medical examiner's office in order to get the victim's standard DNA.

In yet another email from the DNA examiner's office dated September 7, 2021, the victim's DNA standard was still missing, and the DNA examiner's office had not received the sample from the medical examiner's office.

In an email from September 8, 2021, analyst Sara L. Lamb advised Investigator Cundiff that she had not received necessary information when she stated, "an unmarked manila env was inside my mailbox. I was out of the lab the full week of 08/30–09/03 so I do not know when this env arrived. The env was sealed with adhesive and no initials I opened the env, there is paperwork pertaining to the Louisville OCME chain of custody and a blood standard, but no KSP26. There was a letter from Sgt. Investigator Cundiff to the ME which listed the laboratory number, so I logged this as Item 9 for this case and too the item into my custody. It will remain in my custody until a KSP26 is received."

It is clear from this correspondence that the chain of custody may have been broken on this DNA evidence, and Investigator Cundiff still had not submitted the proper KSP26 for the DNA comparison test. So now it is almost six months after the shooting, and DNA testing has not even begun on this evidence. Furthermore, no DNA was ever taken for comparison from any of the other residents of this trailer where the shooting took place.

If the above emails are not disturbing enough, what follows is nothing short of shocking. An email dated October 1, 2021, at 7:20 a.m. from KSP lab technician Megan May to Investigator Cundiff states, "I am the DNA analyst assigned to this case. I was wondering what exactly is needed with exhibit 00010—'black cloth from 9mm Hi-Point'? I see that the gun hasn't been submitted and was wondering if there was a reason this was not submitted? It would be better to swab the actual gun for touch DNA if that was intention for the cloth. The gun would be useful for firearms testing/comparison as well. Please let me know if there is anything additional I should know about these items."

In a follow-up email from Megan May, dated October 1, 2021, she states, "Was the gun submitted to the KSP lab? I'm not seeing it in the BEAST (Kentucky's evidence lab computer system) as an Item that was submitted to firearms. I can still swab the cloth, but I'm asking in case I don't get usable results I could swab the gun unless it's already been tested. If it's been tested already, then it may not be eligible."

In an email response from Investigator Cundiff to Megan May on October 1, 2021, he states: "The gun has been sent to firearms for testing, but the black cloth was wrapped tightly around the gun at the time of finding it. According to accounts of people that knew the suspect had the gun, he kept cloth wrapped around the grip of the gun, and would carry the gun in his waist band. Leading us to believe there would be a high concentration of DNA on the cloth." This instruction should have been clearly made in the initial request for testing of this gun and the cloth—it was not. The ramifications of Investigator Cundiff's failure to submit the evidence properly are not inconsequential.

In an email dated January 28, 2022, from KSP forensic firearms lab specialist Jessica Copeland to Fred B. Crane, she states, "The firearm in the above referenced case was reportedly submitted to AFIS. Would you please forward this evidence to the Eastern Lab for firearm testing when analysis is complete?" It is exasperating to imagine that almost a year later and apparently no DNA or firearms testing has been completed on this 9mm, not to mention no fingerprints were ever produced by the prosecution. This gun should have been sent to the lab for DNA testing first, before any other testing. The other testing for fingerprints and ballistic evidence could have greatly altered or destroyed the DNA. Again, this was not done and was in fact brought out during the trial.

The most concerning email is the one dated June 5, 2023, from Megan May to the prosecutor on this case, Commonwealth Attorney David Dalton, which states, "This email was accidentally sent to another analyst here at the lab, whose name is also Megan. I am the analyst who performed analysis in this case. There are reports under 2 different lab numbers for this case. Lab # 21-C-03131 contains serological and DNA results for exhibits 3 (knife), 10 (cloth form 9mm Hi-Point), 18 (buccal standard from Samuel Baker) and 1 (blood standard from VICTIM'S NAME). Lab #: 21-C-03973 contains DNA results for exhibits 00007 (Hi-Point 9mm pistol), 00008 (9mm live round from Hi-Point pistol) and 00009 (Magazine and 2 live rounds) along with a comparison to the standards in the 21-C-03131 lab #."

The lack of clarity from the investigator has caused, or substantially contributed to, emails and evidence being inadvertently sent to two separate Megans at the lab. Does this mean that there are two 9mm pistols being examined? Have they confused evidence in this case because of the lack of initial direction from Investigator Cundiff on what to do with the evidence? And finally, it was now over two years after the shooting and neither the prosecution nor defense had any real answers on the evidence and testing in this case. At this point the trial was scheduled for July 2023, which was less than a month from the above email. This allowed the prosecutor, who had lost contact with his witness, Ronald Baker, to seek and be granted a much-needed postponement of the trial over the objection of defense counsel.

On July 31, 2023, Pulaski County Deputy Matt Bryant submitted a report in his name and not that of the initial investigator, Cundiff. This was not surprising since the proverbial cat was out of the bag on the evidence room and Investigator Cundiff was a suspect in the missing currency/evidence. In the narrative of his report, he clearly states, among other things, that the Bureau of Alcohol, Tobacco, and Firearms (BATF) had completed its report on August 4, 2023, which was almost two and a half years after the shooting. So, in other words, it only took a month for the BATF to complete its report, but for some still unexplained reason, the Pulaski County Sheriff's Office waited two and a half years to submit the firearm for testing in a murder case. Even more astonishing is the fact that a report regarding this BATF report was not completed by Deputy Bryant until November 15, 2023, almost three years after this shooting. What this report by Deputy Bryant reveals is nothing short of astonishing and probably holds the reason as to why they slow-walked this part of the investigation and changed the investigator from Investigator Cundiff to Deputy Bryant. Here's verbatim how the report reads:

> BATF completed the request on August 4, 2023 and pro-
> duced a Firearms Trace Summary. The summary listed
> the purchaser as Bradford Gene Bryant with an address
> of 40 Doctor Parker Lane, Gray, Kentucky 40734, It list-
> ed his date of birth as [REDACTED FOR BOOK] and a
> state-issued identification card number of [REDACTED
> FOR BOOK]. The summary also showed that the trans-
> action occurred on March 12, 2020, three-hundred and
> seventy-two days prior to the offense. The summary

further showed that Mr. Bryant purchased the pistol at Badwoods Outdoors, 2709 Cumberland Falls Hwy, Corbin, Kentucky 40701.

Through investigation, it was determined that Mr. Bryant is currently employed at B&M Wheel alignment, Corbin KY 40701. I contacted BATF Special Agent (SA) John Barnett and asked if he could interview Mr. Bryant at his place of employment. SA Barnett interviewed Mr. Bryant on august 15, 2023, and a report of his interview with Mr. Bryant appends this supplement. In summary, Mr. Bryant told SA Barnett that he sold the pistol to a male he knows as "Dwayne Loyd" and said that "Dwayne" told him that he was purchasing the pistol for a friend of his that he called "Donovan." Mr. Bryant told SA Barnett that "Dwayne" is in jail in Pulaski County where he is serving five years imprisonment. It was determined that there currently is a David Wayne Lloyd incarcerated on a five – year sentence at Pulaski Jail. A photograph of David Wayne Lloyd was showed to Mr. Bryant, who identified him as the man he knows as "Dwayne Lloyd." Mr. Bryant told SA Barnett that he sold the pistol to Lloyd in the summer of 2020, when he met Lloyd in Corbin and Lloyd paid him $250 and Mr. Bryant gave him the pistol. On August 15, 2023 at approximately 3:25 pm, SA Barnett and I want to Pulaski Jail to interview David Wayne Lloyd. He was shown a photograph of the recovered pistol in his investigation and immediately recognized it as a Hi-Point 9mm as the photograph was being handed to him. He stated he purchased a pistol like that from someone named "Jeff Idle" but he was unsure how the last name is spelled. He said he purchased it from him on Griffin Street where he, Lloyd, used to live.

He said this was approximately five years ago. He said that he might have sold it to a red-haired female named Jessica Johnson who said is approximately thirty to thirty-five years of age. He said this was approximately two years ago. He said that he went to jail and had left some guns in his car in his backpack and that she may have gotten it from there.

As I read this report, several things stood out. First, none of these interviews produced a connection to Sam Baker. Second, the prosecution failed to relinquish the actual BATF report regarding this 9mm to defense counsel. It only provided the sheriff's office version of this report. To any trained investigator, this presented significant concerns. Third, again, why was this BATF investigation not completed immediately after the shooting? Investigator Cundiff could have simply submitted the make, model, and serial number of this 9mm to BATF, and it could have completed this investigation over two years ago, when the memories of witnesses would have been much clearer. And lastly, it demonstrated that a previous owner, who is now a felon serving a five-year sentence, could have very well disposed of this gun in the woods prior to Sam Baker's arrest.

This alone does not completely exonerate Sam Baker, but it comes real close. Here again, the question is why the delay? Was this lack of investigation done on purpose? We pressured the prosecution from July 2023 to March 2024 for the rest of this report. On the Friday before the 2024 trial date, the prosecution supplied a one-page BATF printout showing it had run the gun through its system. The prosecution never supplied any BATF reports or recordings of the interviews BATF had completed on this gun. For obvious reasons, interviews of all witnesses and suspects should have been recorded either by video or audio. The fact that several interviews of alleged prior owners of this gun were taken, but the prosecution could only provide a written summary produced by the Pulaski County Sheriff's Office and the BATF printout was, at best, perfunctory and, at worst, a deliberate concealment of what actually occurred during the interviews.

I know the above reference to numerous documents can become overwhelming and boring; however, the devil is in the details when it comes to proper crime scene investigation and experts. All too often defense attorneys make the mistake of assuming the experts are what they say they are and fail to completely review and challenge their documents and testimony. As the old humorous admonition warns, "never assume because it makes an ass out of *u* and *me*." Fortunately, attorney Jim Cox is not one of those defense attorneys. In a previous murder trial that I refer to as the choking gum case, I worked as an investigator with Jim and we uncovered that a medical examiner out of Frankfort was not as qualified as she had initially been presented. In that case, which involved the suspected murder of a toddler, the medical examiner had never examined a child before and had never passed the required testing to be a licensed Kentucky medical examiner. Yet the supervisors in the Kentucky medical examiner's office allowed this woman to examine this child without any supervision. Further, we uncovered that she followed no standard scientific evidence protocols, much like the ballistics examiner in the Faubush-Norfleet Road murder case. She had no outside peer group assessment, other than her Frankfort supervisors. It was also discovered during the chocking gum trial, that Kentucky medical examiners do not follow the accepted standard protocol of transmitting real time audio or video recordings of their work as they are performing it. There were only her notes after the fact. As would be expected in this chocking gum case, the medical examiner botched her examination and was later let go by the Kentucky Office of the Medical Examiner.

Because of this, and many other mistakes in the choking gum case, our clients were justifiably awarded a second trial. When Jim Cox crossed-examined this Frankfort medical examiner on the stand, her inexperience and lack of qualifications were revealed. Later I found her crying in the hall. Part of me felt sorry for her; however, who I really felt sorry for were the two parents who served two years in prison for a murder that was never a murder in the first place.

After the second trial of the choking gum murder case, our clients went home. The sad truth about this case is the fact that it involved two very young teenagers, eighteen and nineteen years old, who spent over two years in jail and were not even allowed to attend their child's funeral—yet they were innocent. What was made clear in the second trial was that the child had choked on gum. There were numerous documents that clearly stated this, and the emergency room doctor even testified to the fact that he pulled a big wad of gum out of the child's mouth and saved it as evidence. There were a lot more mistakes in the criminal investigation by the cops and the Frankfort experts in this case. But the point I am making is that had we not carefully reviewed and questioned this evidence and the experts, those two teenagers would have spent most of their lives in prison for a murder they did not commit. In fact, they would have remained imprisoned for a murder that was not even a murder, but factually a horrible accident. The devil is in the details.

In this Faubush-Norfleet murder case, there were many more FUBAR mistakes by the investigators. One would think that these and other mistakes, combined with the abuses of the sheriff's office evidence room and the distrust of Investigator Cundiff on this case, would surely cause reasonable doubt in the jury's mind as to who really shot the victim.

What the jury was not allowed to hear was that this trial was originally scheduled to start in April 2023 and then again in July 2023.These postponements were through no fault of the defendant Sam Baker or his defense team. In the July 2023 hearing, just days before the trial was scheduled to begin, suspect Ronald Baker disappeared and could not be found. The judge had to issue a material witness warrant to get him to trial. In other words, Ronald Baker ran from this trial but the jury never got to hear this. This would have made Ronald Baker's testimony even more unreliable. Given that his testimony was the only real evidence they had, it could have altered the jury's perception of him immensely. However, this was not allowed to be conveyed to the jury. I found this highly prejudicial to Sam Baker, our client.

Most importantly, the prosecution never really brought forward any real motive for Sam Baker to be the shooter. It only produced the testimony of suspect Ronald Baker, a previously convicted drug dealer who was admittedly high on methamphetamine the night of the shooting. The same Ronald Baker who had to be brought in by a material witness warrant after he ran from the July 2023 scheduled trial.

This case finally went to trial in May 2024 after numerous postponements through no fault of the defendant. The defendant, Sam Baker, was found guilty after a one-week trial. He was sentenced to life in prison. Before the trial, the defendant had been out on bond with an ankle monitor awaiting his trial. Just days before his trial was to begin in December 2023, Sam Baker cut off his ankle monitor and fled. He stole a vehicle and a gun and fled to Kansas with his girlfriend, a former prison guard at the Pulaski County Detention Center, where they met. I am convinced that if Sam Baker had not run, this trial could have ended very differently. When the jury heard testimony of how Sam Baker had run, they were highly prejudiced by it. The prosecution conflated Sam Baker's running with the murder charge to prejudicially convince the jury of his guilt in both. Remember, suspect Ronald Baker had run too, causing a delay in the trial, but the jury never heard about this. Had the jury known this, perhaps it would have elevated Ronald Baker to the same amount of suspicion as his son.

Despite the outcome of the criminal trial of Sam Baker, what came out of this trial and defense investigation was nothing short of shocking and a story certainly worth telling. In the defense's closing arguments, attorney Jim Cox talked to the jury while I listed on large poster boards the numerous doubts as to Sam Baker's guilt. We listed thirty-eight reasonable doubts as to why the jury should acquit Sam Baker. In Kentucky, it only takes "a reasonable doubt" to acquit. They had thirty-eight very reasonable doubts, and they still sentenced Sam Baker to life in prison.

After working for both sides, defense and prosecution for over forty years, I am convinced of one thing: cases are usually won or lost in closing arguments. The old saying "first impressions are lasting impressions," I believe is incorrect. What my training and experience has taught me is that a person's last impression of someone is the impression that lasts. When you leave that person, their last emotion about you is what will resonate, not what they remember from a week ago. When the jury's last thought of the case before they deliberate is a positive emotional connection with the prosecutor, and that positive feeling carries straight into the deliberation room, that becomes influence. When the prosecution is allowed to go last, it is an extreme advantage for the prosecution to have the last word with the jury. This is highly prejudicial to the defense. The defense has no opportunity to counter any misstatements or misleading arguments presented by the prosecution. The defense may object to the misstatements and misleading arguments, but by that time the genie is already out of the bottle, and the jury has already heard the comments. At best, the judge will reprimand the prosecution with a stern admonition but rarely any substantive explanation will be conveyed to the jury on why the prosecutorial statement was incorrect, except that it was legally inadmissible. Such judicial admonitions rarely, if ever, convince a jury to disregard what was said. In fact, they frequently capitalize on the statement for jurors who did not comprehend the statement when the prosecutor initially said it. This happens all too often in criminal cases.

Despite the outcome of this particular case, I felt that it was extremely important to document the following: (1) a biased investigation that only pursued evidence to support the guilt of one individual, rather than an investigation that properly collected evidence that impartially eliminated all suspects except one; (2) exposure of an extraordinarily compromised evidence room that was repeatedly subjected to burglaries, thefts, and possible evidence manipulations; and (3) the possible cover-up that ensued. Despite what anyone thinks about the defendant Sam Baker or the victim in this case, both individuals and their families deserved a fair, complete, and competent investigation into what happened. Clearly that was not done. The body cams alone demonstrated questionable law enforcement actions that defendants and victims alike should find unacceptable in any case, but especially in a high-profile murder case. This coupled with the incredible admissions made by the sheriff and the other deputies during this trial should serve as a textbook case for what not to do during a crime scene investigation. It is important to remember that a conviction does not validate a bad investigation. Oftentimes a bad investigation ensures a conviction.

This case, above all of the numerous others that I have investigated, should be used as an educational tool in police academies and training sessions. I have shown the body cam footage to defense attorneys, prosecutors, and other seasoned and extremely competent investigators. They all agreed that this crime scene investigation was one of the worst they had ever seen. This type of injustice is precisely how the innocent get wrongfully convicted and the guilty go free.

Moreover, when law enforcement does not possess the resources, equipment, training, and experience to process these complicated crime scenes and investigations, they need to put their egos aside and allow agencies that do have the resources equipment, training, and experience to step in and take over. Far too often this is not happening in law enforcement. This frustrates prosecutors and makes their job extremely difficult.

Interestingly enough, at the Kentucky Prosecutors Conference in August 2024,Commonwealth Attorney David L. Dalton gave an entire presentation to Kentucky prosecutors with the heading "A Tale of 2 Evidence Rooms." As you will recall, Mr. Dalton was the prosecutor on both the Faubush-Norfleet murder case (Commonwealth v. Sam Baker) and the Somerset PD Captain Mike Correll criminal case, both of which involved missing evidence/currency as detailed in previous chapters. In this ethics-style presentation, Mr. Dalton outlined the Pulaski County and Somerset police departments evidence room debacles, how he as a prosecutor handled the situations, and what he recommended to other prosecutors in handling these types of situations. I must admit that the recommendations he gave at this conference on turning over discovery and getting everything to the judge were actually quite good. So perhaps the glass is not half empty, and some educational guidance has resulted from the highly defective evidence rooms.

Chapter 7

J. S. FLYNN: THE "CALL ME DADDY" CLERK

In March 2024, the Kentucky Supreme Court ruled to remove Circuit Court Clerk Joseph "J.S." Flynn from his office. This was by no means an easy task in Kentucky, to remove an elected official. This was after a lengthy investigation by the Kentucky Administrative Office of the Courts (AOC) and a jaw-dropping three-day hearing before a special commissioner (judge). The job of the circuit court clerk (clerk) in each county is to manage the court records, schedule juries, and receive court fines and costs for the court of justice. This requires the hiring of deputy clerks to assist the clerk.

On March 23, 2022, Tabitha Burnett was a deputy clerk in the Pulaski circuit court clerk's office who filed a complaint against Flynn with the Kentucky AOC. She alleged several incidents in which Flynn engaged in inappropriate workplace behavior. Several other allegations were then brought forward by other deputy clerks. This set off an investigation by the AOC into Flynn's actions. The Kentucky Supreme Court placed Flynn on paid leave while the AOC investigated these complaints.

The special commissioner then held the three-day hearing beginning on May 10, 2023.

On July 7, 2023, the special commissioner filed her findings of fact, conclusions of law, and recommendations with the court. She concluded that Flynn created a hostile work environment by physically assaulting Burnett in a vehicle incident, reaching under her dress in the workplace, otherwise flirting with and touching her in the office against her wishes, and making sexual comments to her. The special commissioner found that, among other things, Flynn also created a hostile work environment by pinching other female employees on the back below their bra while making statements such as "let daddy feel your bacon" and asking them to call him "Daddy." Flynn acknowledges pinching employees to "scare" them but denies making reference to "bacon."

I attended this three-day hearing and what I witnessed was nothing short of disturbing. The Kentucky Judge Advocate General's (JAG) office prosecuted this administrative hearing. One of the first witnesses was Tabitha Burnett. Burnett testified that Flynn had pressured her over time into having a sexual relationship with him by holding her job over her head. At one point she stated, "I was a single mom trying to raise my kids. I needed this job and he wore me down. So I just finally gave in." Flynn acknowledged, by his own admission, that he engaged in a brief sexual relationship with Burnett, his subordinate, and failed to properly report this obvious conflict of interest. Burnett testified that she and coworker Hanna Garner went to lunch with Flynn. On the return drive back from lunch, Flynn was sitting in the back seat. Burnett stated that Flynn pulled her from the front seat into the back seat of the vehicle, forcefully kissed her on the face and neck, pulled up her shirt and kissed her breast, and exposed himself, all while Burnett and Garner were screaming for him stop.

In other incidents, Burnett testified that for years Flynn would rub her back, hair, and legs in the office in front of coworkers and the public. She further testified that in one particular incident, Flynn put his hand up her dress in front of her coworker Ashley Haste and bailiff Junior Fortenberry. Burnett testified that the day before she filed her complaint, Flynn pushed her out of an office, slammed the door in her face, slammed the door in Haste's face, and then proceeded to curse and yell in Haste's face, causing a customer to cry. Burnett testified that she was afraid to go to work because she felt threatened and was verbally and sexually harassed by Flynn.

I found Burnett's testimony very credible.

Ashley Haste, the secretary for District Judge Lawless, also testified at this hearing. Haste had worked as a support specialist for the Pulaski District Court for fourteen years. Haste testified that she was walking by Flynn one day and overheard a conversation about a vehicle and asked who Flynn was talking about. Haste testified that Flynn replied, in a hostile tone, "What the fuck are you talking about! No one was talking to you." Haste also testified to a situation where the clerk's office had received an unusual package and feared what it may contain. Out of an abundance of caution, Haste reported it to her chain of command and was afraid to open it. To this, Flynn responded by rubbing the package on his crouch and then stating, "This will give you a real reason to fear the package."

Haste also testified that she had witnessed Flynn rubbing women's shoulders and playing with their hair. Additionally, Flynn had grabbed her by the back and said, "Come here and let Daddy feel your bacon" and repeatedly told her to "call me Daddy." She made it clear that she didn't want to be alone in the clerk's office with Flynn. Haste had also witnessed an incident where Flynn put his hand up the dress of Tabitha Burnett while in a judge's chambers. When Flynn did this, Haste told Flynn, "You do know there are cameras in here," and Flynn responded, "We'll give them something to look at." This was also witnessed by bailiff Junior Fortenberry.

Haste testified that Flynn would openly brag in the office about how he slept with other women and his wife. She also testified that on one occasion, Flynn told her to "get out of my fucking office" and that was when she decided to tell Judge Lawless what was going on. Judge Lawless responded by later confronting Flynn; his testimony regarding this is covered below.

It is important to note that much of the behavior Haste testified to was also in earshot of the public. I found Haste extremely credible in her testimony as well.

Chief Deputy Clerk Frank Turner Barrett testified at this hearing as well. He testified that he witnessed Flynn being disrespectful toward the female clerks. He also witnessed a very inappropriate sexual joke or comment by Flynn in front of Hanna Garner where the punch line was "spit or swallow." He testified that the office was much more functional and efficient when Flynn wasn't there. He stated that when Flynn was there, everyone was on edge.

Pulaski County sheriff and bailiff Junior Fortenberry also testified at this hearing. He was present and witnessed the incident where Flynn put his hand up Tabitha Burnett's dress. He was shocked at this incident and thought it was disgusting. He witnessed Flynn yelling at clerks and cussing at clerks where customers could hear. He overheard Flynn making sexual jokes and comments with the people around him, all of whom seemed disgusted and embarrassed. I found Fortenberry extremely credible in his testimony.

Deputy Clerk Hanna Garner also testified. She stated that she witnessed Flynn routinely using harsh language in the office where the public could hear. She also witnessed Flynn rubbing clerks' shoulders and hair, even though they didn't seem to enjoy it. Garner was the driver when she witnessed Flynn forcibly pulling Tabitha Burnett from the front passenger seat to the back seat. She stated that Burnett was not consenting to this and was screaming for him to stop. She stated that she could not see everything that was going on in the back seat, that her view was blocked as she was trying to drive and look into the rearview mirror. She could tell Burnett was struggling, and Garner finally screamed very loud for him to stop and that's when it ended. She also testified that Burnett had confided in her that she did not want to have a relationship with Flynn and she was very upset. She testified that since Flynn was suspended, the office environment was not as anxious.

I found Garner to be the most credible witness of all. When she was on the stand talking about the incident where Flynn pulled Burnett into the back seat of the car as she was screaming, you could see that Garner was reliving the event while on the stand. If she wanted to lie, she could have said she also saw Flynn expose himself and grope Burnett. She did not. She recounted what a reasonable person would probably see in a rearview mirror as they were trying to drive. In my opinion, Flynn was lucky this didn't cause Garner to wreck and injure someone. The real question is why wasn't Flynn charged with criminal assault? Here again, the good ol' boy/"who's your daddy" politics were probably at play.

The next witness was Deputy Clerk Kasey Cassada. She testified that she had witnessed Flynn's angry attitude and outburst, and Flynn cussing and screaming at his staff in front of customers. She also testified to the fact that Flynn only came to the office a couple of times a week on average. She witnessed Burnett repeatedly doing her best to thwart Flynn's advances toward her and him getting angry. She witnessed an incident where Ashley Haste wanted to get files and Flynn got irate and yelled, "This is my fucking office." Cassada stated that she had an attorney on the phone and Flynn was so loud that she placed the attorney on hold. After this incident she also witnessed Judge Lawless come downstairs and confront Flynn. Lawless stated to Flynn, "You're not going to cuss [out] my employees," among other things. Cassada stated that the confrontation between Flynn and Judge Lawless was very intense and that Haste was very upset. She stated that Flynn would cuss and use the f-word routinely in front of the public. When asked why she didn't file a complaint against Flynn, she indicated that she knew Flynn would make life and work difficult for her. She stated that work was easier since Flynn was suspended, that there was "no more drama."

Cassada recounted an incident where she was on the phone helping an elderly gentleman by talking him through a website for a driver's license. Flynn yelled at her while she was on the phone and said, "That's not your fucking job. If he was that stupid, he doesn't need a license." Again, I found Cassada's testimony to be credible.

Deputy Clerk Raynette Meece then testified. She witnessed Flynn's temper and him routinely yelling and cussing. She said they had a name for it: a "Flynn Fit." He hit the copy machine with his hand in one of these fits. She testified that it was fairly common for Flynn to treat employees with disrespect. She also testified that Flynn only came into the office about three times a week, that he was gone more than he was there. She stated that, "the mood was better when he wasn't there. You knew you weren't going to be embarrassed that day." She witnessed Flynn making sexual comments about customers and their physical appearance. He would make statements like how he would like to "fuck her." She witnessed him routinely and inappropriately touching women in the office, grabbing their backs and calling it his "back bacon." She witnessed Flynn routinely touching Burnett in the office and placing his hand on her upper thigh. She also witnessed Flynn calling Burnett a "bitch and whore."

Meece also witnessed the incident between Flynn and Haste where Haste was just trying to get her files. Flynn yelled at Haste to "get the fuck out of my office." She then witnessed the confrontation that followed between Judge Lawless and Flynn. Flynn admitted to Meece that he knew that he "messed up" that day.

Judge Scott Lawless, retired district judge, testified next. He testified that he had been hearing complaints about Flynn. Judge Lawless had witnessed Flynn pinch Ashley Haste as she jerked away. She later stated she was disgusted. She told Lawless that she didn't want Flynn in their office or to be alone with him. Lawless also observed statements online from Flynn calling Burnett, his deputy clerk, a whore. Judge Lawless stated that he was angry about the incident with Haste. Lawless stated that when he confronted Flynn, "I thought he was going to hit me." When Lawless told Flynn, "Do not talk to my staff like that," Flynn responded, "I'll talk to whomever I want however I want."

It is important to note that soon after Judge Lawless confronted Flynn and stood up for the clerks, a stream of people wanted to file reports against Flynn. As I watched Judge Lawless's testimony, it became apparent to me that the clerks finally felt like someone would believe them and stand up for them. This was why they finally felt more comfortable to file complaints on Flynn.

Last to testify was J.S. Flynn. His story was not surprising. Everyone was lying but him. He denied ever cussing at clerks. He denied the "call me Daddy" quote. He surprisingly admitted to touching the ladies' back and hair. He stated, "I didn't hear any of them complain." He did admit to cussing at Ashley Haste and understood why Lawless was mad.

Shortly before this hearing, the judge issued an order stating that no one involved in this hearing should be posting anything on social media. This was to thwart any intimidation that may result from those type of posts. Now keep in mind, this wasn't a suggestion; this was an order from a judge. Yet when Flynn took the stand, he admitted, unapologetically, to posting just before this hearing a video of Johnny Cash accompanied by statements that anyone with half a brain would interpret as threatening. Here are some of the lyrics to this song:

> You can run on for a long time
> Run on for a long time
> Run on for a long time
> Sooner or later God'll cut you down
> Sooner or later God'll cut you down
> Go tell that long tongue liar
>
> Go and tell that midnight rider
> Tell the rambler, the gambler, the back biter
> Tell 'em that God's gonna cut 'em down
> Tell 'em that God's gonna cut 'em down

As I am writing about this J.S. Flynn case, I simply have one word for these clerks: lawsuit. You know in my over forty years of experience in many types of criminal and civil cases, this has to be one of the most egregious, over-the-top civil cases I have ever witnessed. I am equally shocked that there were no criminal charges ever filed against Flynn and that no husbands, boyfriends, or partners ever showed up to beat the crap out of him.

What was astonishing to me was just how long and how much this guy got away with before being sanctioned in any way. The female supervisor who testified for Flynn during this hearing testified that for years she witnessed him engaging in this "creeper" behavior, and she thought it was fine. She actually testified that she wanted him back as her boss. As the clerk's supervisor, she had a duty to protect her subordinates and a duty to report Flynn, which she never did previously. As I watched her testify, one thought ran through my head: she should be removed from her job right along with Flynn. This never happened. Mid-level managers who do not protect their employees from this type of egregious behavior are as bad as the bosses they cover for.

At least the Kentucky Supreme Court had the good sense to re-move him from office—after a yearlong paid vacation on the taxpayers, of course. Flynn should have been made to pay this back to the tax-payers. Thus far, he has not. For the May 2024 primary, Flynn paid to put his name back on the ballot for clerk. Unfortunately, no one ran against Flynn in the primary and only a write-in candidate entered the race just weeks before the November 2024 election. Flynn was elected back into this office by the voters. Here again our Kentucky legislature is asleep behind the wheel. It could have passed a law basically requiring that once an elected official was removed from office by the Kentucky Supreme Court for any type of egregious behavior, they cannot run for office again.

Again, you just can't make this shit up.

Chapter 8

IN CLOSING

Becoming a public official or a police officer should be looked upon as a gift. You should see it as an opportunity to do something good in your life, something good for society. You have the chance to be part of something bigger than just yourself. Sam Rayburn, former speaker of the house, once said, "Any jackass can kick down a barn, but it takes a carpenter to build one." I am a person who has devoted a lifetime to investigative work. I have prepared myself by attending countless training academies and programs, and I have earned advanced degrees. I have grown my expertise by applying that training in various employments in the US Army, the federal government as a Special Agent, and in civilian investigative jobs. Even with these skills, I freely concede that I may not necessarily be equipped as a wordsmith. However, wordsmiths are not equipped to uncover the many nefarious activities that I have exposed during my career.

I write about the fraud, waste, greed, incompetence, and cronyism that I have uncovered because exposure of those things is the only disinfectant. While those things can never be completely eradicated, they certainly can be ameliorated by good people who have the courage and initiative to confront those in power who are committing these acts or condone them through their inaction. Consequently, I am writing this book not to demonize, embarrass, or besmirch any individuals but rather as a change agent.

Again, I want to make it clear that while it may seem that I am picking on Pulaski County in this book, there are other stories in other Kentucky counties that are worse. For example, our news program, *Truth or Politics*, was one of the first local news agencies to report on a shocking story in Letcher County, Kentucky. In September 2024 the Letcher County sheriff fatally gunned down District Judge Kevin Mullins in his chambers inside the Letcher County courthouse. This was after a conversation between the two inside the courthouse. This shooting was caught on camera inside the judge's chambers. Here again we have a small rural community where everyone knows each other and many are related in some way. Shawn "Micky" Stines was the sheriff seen in this shocking video gunning down this judge, and the video appears to show the judge begging for his life. Apparently this was not the first crime documented in this judge's chambers at night, after the courthouse was closed to the general public.

The sheriff's bailiff, Ben Fields, was previously prosecuted and pled guilty for extorting sex from female detainees in exchange for not having to pay for ankle monitors. Bailiff Ben Fields pleaded guilty in January 2024 to third-degree rape, third-degree sodomy, tampering with a prisoner's monitoring device, and second-degree perjury, according to court records. Not surprisingly, this bailiff case of sextortion became a lawsuit on behalf of the women/victims of this bailiff. The ankle monitor system that allows individuals to stay out of jail is virtually unregulated in the state of Kentucky, like so many other things, including evidence rooms. Sometimes the companies or individuals who get the contracts to control these ankle monitors are cronies of the local good ol' boys in power. There are many conflicts of interest regarding this system, and, if you have money, you can get the monitor and stay out of jail. If you are poor and cannot afford an ankle monitor, you are more vulnerable to what happened in this case—sex for freedom. Again, our legislature's lackadaisical approach to this issue in Kentucky tends to encourage bad behavior.

An audio recording of a subsequent interview of one of Ben Fields's female victims was released by the Kentucky attorney general's office. This victim told investigators that the man who had the video claimed to have numerous similar videos of other people that were on VHS tapes, but she said she had only seen one of the videos. During the attorney general office's interview with the victim in that civil case in 2022, she claimed she had seen a video of Judge Mullins having sex with a woman in his chambers at the courthouse. Despite this allegation, Judge Mullins was never charged with anything related to this allegation.

According to the administrative office of the courts, there were additional cameras installed in the Letcher County courthouse after the victim's federal lawsuit against Bailiff Fields in 2022. The cameras were placed at the request of "the judges, circuit court clerk, and Sheriff Stines." In this victim's federal lawsuit, Sheriff Stines is named for failing to investigate sexual assaults within his department. Just three days before Sheriff Stines shot Judge Mullins, he gave a deposition in this lawsuit in which he was accused of failing to investigate a deputy sheriff, Bailiff Fields, who sexually abused a woman in the judge's chambers.

Although police have yet to officially provide a motive for the sheriff's shooting of Judge Mullins, allegations surrounding the relationship between the judge and sheriff have been swirling around for months. One of these allegations involved the sheriff's daughter and the judge's cell phone. Sheriff Stines had previously served as a bailiff in Judge Mullins's court, and the two were longtime friends. The defense for Sheriff Stines is not denying that the shooting happened but is alleging that the sheriff did so during an "extreme emotional disturbance." As of December 2024, investigation continues into this fatal shooting.

When our elected officials and law enforcement are allowed to operate with impunity, with little to no checks and balances, the results can be devastating. What I also found to be very disturbing, especially in Pulaski County, was the level of fear the good citizens, honest cops, and honest public officials have of speaking truth to power to some public officials. The clique that controls the power in Pulaski County has sent clear messages to others who dare to challenge them. Their empirical knowledge has taught them that questioning this clique is a risk to their jobs or even their freedom. The message is clear: either fall in line or be ostracized out of a job or business.

The fear in this community is very real. It causes citizens to fear questioning their leadership when leadership desperately needs questioning. It should concern everyone that it took over three years, a documentary, numerous city council meetings, feature articles in the local newspaper, and approximately seventy million gallons of toxic waste for citizens to become concerned enough to actually show up and demand an end to the leachate problem. Falling in line, going along to get along, and not making waves when your very health and freedoms are at stake is damn dangerous. This is not the exception in Kentucky—it seems to be the norm. While citizens will rail against politicians like Biden and Trump at the national level on social media, they are complacent or just plain fearful of learning about and standing up against what is going on in their own backyards.

At the very least, there is clear evidence of extreme cronyism at play not only in Pulaski County but statewide. Throughout my over forty years of education, training, and experience, I can attest to the fact that cronyism breeds corruption. A large part of this equation is people who crave power desperately enough to compromise their integrity just to be near it and receive its rewards. If they cannot gain power legitimately, through hard work and education, they will become sycophants to public officials in powerful positions. It is almost as though they foolishly think that by standing next to power, it somehow makes them equally powerful through some type of bizarre osmosis. What these cronies and minions fail to realize is that the public officials they are cozying up to rarely see them as more than useful idiots.

This abuse of power has little to no oversight and only seems to get addressed after it completely breaks down or someone more powerful is harmed by it. This can also be seen with many politically appointed boards that wield enormous power in Kentucky. Rarely is this reported by local and statewide news outlets, because they have become so polarized and political that most reporters have become talking heads. It is simply not in their interest to expose unwelcome truths about public officials who are also purchasing large, high-dollar ads from these very same news organizations. The corrupt insist upon favorable news for which they have paid, oftentimes with public funds. In other words, they simply get the news they pay for.

The mainstream media being more political than factual in their reporting is a recipe for disaster. The underreporting on bad or corrupt law enforcement and public officials in Kentucky is astonishing. Local papers and even larger community papers are not incentivized in challenging or questioning law enforcement leadership and public officials in Kentucky. I have been contacted anonymously by reporters from other newspapers and agencies who give me leads and stories they are simply not allowed to cover themselves. I have lost track of the number of times reporters have given me information and told me, "I can't cover this, I have to live here."Again, this is why whistleblower laws and press shield laws matter. If any state has weak whistleblower and press shield laws and/or refuses to enforce them, then the result is a loss of the checks and balances system we have in this country. Even when the laws are in place, if courts do not uphold them, then we are in even greater danger. This is occurring in some areas of Kentucky, and I fear in many other states.

One time after I had received leads on yet another corruption story, I asked attorney Jim Cox, "What the hell, am I just a magnet for this shit or what? It seems like everywhere I turn there's more and more corruption!" Jim's answer was disturbing. He said, "No, Darlene, it's just that prevalent, and because of what you have been through, you see it where others do not."

The Kentucky legislature needs to enact strict, updated laws and then mandate enforcement of these laws through the courts in the following areas: whistleblower protection laws, press shield laws, campaign finance laws, evidence room regulations, conflict of interest laws to appointed boards, and strong conflict of interest laws regarding the contract bidding process involving taxpayer money.

The lack of checks and balances regarding all of these areas of law in Kentucky is the fault of our legislature and the courts. The state of Kentucky does not require official data collection by the police or the publication of that data.

Case in point: two days before Christmas 2024, members of the London City Police apparently went to the wrong address, late at night, to execute a search warrant for a weedeater and space heater. They forced entry into an innocent man's home, then shot and killed him. It was not until three days later that the department came out with the report that the resident, sixty-three-year-old Douglas Harless, pointed a gun at the officers. If the officers had simply waited until the next day, this fatal mistake may very well have been avoided.

There was absolutely no reason and no exigent circumstances for this police department to rush out, in the dead of night, and serve this warrant over a few hundred dollars of merchandise. In my reading of the reports thus far, numerous red flags immediately come to mind. Clearly, proper protocol for verification of the address for this warrant was not followed. There should have been a reconnaissance of the location where an officer could have run the license plates of any vehicle at the location for further verification. Proper reconnaissance in daylight would also have made it easier to actually see the address numbers on the residence. In the light of day, proper observation could have discerned that this was an old man who probably did not fit any description of the suspected thief. Property, electric, and water records should have been checked for this address and physically matched to the location via reconnaissance. I understand that these things take time, but like it or not, that is the job. Sometimes the best thing to do in any situation is to simply slow down and think.

The other silent question is who was supervising these officers? Any well-trained and experienced supervisor should have been questioning the affiant officer on this search warrant as to what they had undertaken to ensure this was the correct address. What should have also been questioned is why the rush and why so late at night. There appears to be no exigent circumstances surrounding this stolen property that would have warranted a late-night, rushed execution of a search warrant. Any law enforcement official with proper training and experience knows that nighttime raids and execution of warrants increases the danger exponentially. The tragic result of what appears to be incompetence has devastated this entire community. This is now being investigated by the KSP. This is just one of several sad stories regarding obvious police negligence in Kentucky that could have had a different ending with better training, proper oversight, improved regulations, and transparency.

Unfortunately, what is happening in Kentucky as a whole is a microcosm of what is happening all across this country. I mean really, do you think this country got $36 trillion in debt by honest politicians and honest judges protecting an honest system? The answer is no. The system is rigged and the money changers in both political parties have already won, I fear. When our elected officials at the state and federal level weakened almost all of the campaign finance laws in America and the courts upheld these rulings, bribery became legal.

Further, in February 2024 I was part of a public educational panel at our local library entitled "An Evening of Journalism." We had four seasoned journalists on this panel. Two of them were editors of their papers and one was a former, well-known journalist and television producer of a Kentucky television news station. One of the best and most shocking comments/concerns relayed to this panel from the audience was stated by my husband, Austin Price. He told of how when he was young, he was taught that citizens of Russia knew their state-run media was nothing more than propaganda. However, the Russian citizens learned how to recognize the propaganda and glean the facts. Austin further stated "that's where we are in this country with the left wing and right wing media. We watch both, we weed out the propaganda and figure out that the truth is somewhere in the middle. I think it's shocking that now in this country we have to watch our news with the same skepticism as the citizens of Russia."

The results of much of what is written in this book is an atmosphere of cronyism and outright corruption in this state. I was warned by several attorney friends of mine and honest elected officials that I had better not state these truths in this book. This is a standard type of statement anytime I dare to question anyone in power, be it law enforcement, the courts, Kentucky's boards, and/or Kentucky's legislature.

It is the job of any investigative reporter to do just that—to dig up evidence and question power. When kind folks try to warn me about these underlying and sometimes not so subtle threats, I simply reply, "That's okay, let them come. I'll just make them the topic of my next news story or book."

Solutions/Recommendations

Although I have covered these solutions throughout the body of this book, I would like to reiterate these recommendations:

- Liquid leachate from landfills should not be brought into the state of Kentucky and processed through wastewater treatment plants. Virtually none of these plants are equipped to properly filter out PFOs, PFOAs, and/or asbestos. The multibillion dollar industry of landfills should provide treatment plants for leachate at the site of the landfills. This industry rakes in billions and billions of dollars of profit each year and can afford to treat leachate at the site, yet it has chosen to risk the drinking water of millions of Americans and wildlife for profit. Our state lawmakers must pass laws to produce positive change and then enforce these laws.

- State lawmakers must pass meaningful laws and regulations regarding the inspections of police evidence rooms. No evidence room in the state of Kentucky should go for more than two years without proper inspection. These inspectors must be well trained in proper evidence room protocol and must not have any conflicts of interest as inspectors. These laws/regulations must then be rigorously enforced by the attorney general's office.

- State lawmakers must pass meaningful laws and regulations requiring that no officer, sheriff's deputy, constable, or volunteer deputy will be given the authority to carry weapons, conduct investigations, initiate traffic stops, or engage in deadly force without proper training and experience. This must include, at the very least, the completion of a certified police academy of some kind, including but not limited to federal law enforcement training institutes.

- State lawmakers must pass laws and regulations that allow well-trained, former federal law enforcement officials (e.g., DEA, FBI, BATF, IRS, US Army CID, US Air Force OSI, US Navy NIS, etc.) to apply for and be accepted as law enforcement officials in the state of Kentucky. The fact that a volunteer deputy with absolutely no training can carry a badge and gun while many better trained and experienced former federal agents of the law cannot be automatically certified here in Kentucky is nothing more than politics—dangerous politics. This alone would save taxpayers millions of dollars because these fully trained and experienced federal agents would need little to no additional training.

- State lawmakers must pass meaningful laws and regulations regarding the minimum standards to run for the office of sheriff. Law enforcement leadership in the state of Kentucky should be some of the most qualified, not simply a popularity contest.

- State lawmakers must pass meaningful laws and regulations regarding the minimum standards for the selection of the office of chief of police for each city. The political bodies (e.g., city councils and/or mayors) appointing these positions should be required by the state to have some of the most qualified. Further, there must be no conflicts of interest regarding this selection process.

- State lawmakers must pass meaningful laws and regulations regarding the removal of elected officials by the AOC and the Kentucky Supreme Court. Once an elected official has engaged in conduct so egregious that they have been removed from office, laws must be in place forbidding them from seeking the same or another office. This too will save the taxpayers money in preventing what will most certainly be preventable lawsuits.

- State lawmakers must pass stricter laws and regulations regarding the use of taxpayer money for personal use by public officials (e.g., using the city credit card for resort vacations and potential travel for campaigning). Absolutely no taxpayer money should be allowed to be spent on the campaign of any elected official. There are some laws currently in place; however, these laws are not being enforced uniformly. Laws and regulations are not worth the paper they are written on if they are not vigorously enforced.

- State lawmakers must pass stricter laws and regulations regarding the use of taxpayer money for private enterprises that personally benefit elected officials and politically appointed board members (e.g., fake private universities). Again, although some laws and regulations do exist, the current laws are not being enforced and need to be improved upon. The current conflicts of interest that exist regarding the use of taxpayer money for private entities and interest in Kentucky is nothing short of astonishing and fosters misappropriation and malappropriation.

- State lawmakers must pass stricter laws and regulations regarding these politically appointed boards that have tremendous power over jobs, contracts, issuing fines, issuing permits, issuing licenses, certifying police officers, and holding hearings. I could write another book on the many conflicts of interest and lack of expertise that exist on some of these boards that reek of self-dealing and cronyism. Some examples of these boards are the Education Professional Standards Board (EPSB), the Kentucky

Law Enforcement Council, the Kentucky Boxing and Wrestling Commission (KBWC), and the Kentucky Board of Embalmers and Funeral Directors, just to name a few. No one should be granted an appointment to these boards without clear vetting of conflicts of interest and confirmation of expertise. Many of these positions are simply political appointments of the current governor. Although some regulations do exist, these regulations are not being enforced and are not strong enough.

- State lawmakers must pass stricter laws and regulations regarding the issuing of contracts at the state and municipal level. While there are some laws and regulations regarding conflicts of interests and abuse of the taxpayers' money, these are not being adequately enforced, especially on these political boards. Far too much of the taxpayers' money is going only to selective private industry projects, with little to no oversight. These private companies are then more than helpful in funding the political campaigns of the elected officials who approve these contracts. The leadership in Frankfort is well aware of the cronyism and conflicts that exist, and nothing is being done about it.

- State lawmakers must develop, pass laws, and fund some type of public corruption taskforce. What should happen as a result of the mountain of evidence brought forward in the *Truth or Politics* news series and in this book is that these glaring deficiencies should be taken seriously by not only the leadership in Kentucky law enforcement but by state office holders as well. The Kentucky attorney general and the governor's office need to construct a public corruption task force. It needs to be staffed by solid investigators or Special Agents from outside of Kentucky (DEA, FBI, BATF, US Treasury, IRS, US Marshals Service), the attorney general's office, the state auditor's office, the state police, and the governor's office. There needs to be outsiders who have no conflicts of interests. Oftentimes it takes an outsider to be more objective about corrections that need to be made inside. This task force needs to concentrate its efforts on, and only on, accusations of possible waste, fraud, abuse of authority, malfeasance, and corruption of any law enforcement or public officials. This task force needs to have the utmost transparency and regular briefings to both the governor's office and the attorney general's office, each having equal control and oversight—with an emphasis on oversight!

- State lawmakers must pass meaningful laws and regulations regarding standards for selection of instructors in police academies. In the Kentucky police academies, there needs to be more of a diverse pool of instructors, not just mostly retired, white, male state police officers. While KSP does train its officers better than most, many still do not have advanced training and knowledge in processing crime scenes. More experienced, well-trained agents from other agencies like the FBI, DEA, US Treasury, US Marshals, US Army CID, U.S. Air Force OSI, and BATF need to be hired as instructors at these academies. For the most part, these agencies have Special Agents who possess

advanced, extensive training and experience that sur-
passes what most of the KSP officers have to offer.

- State lawmakers must pass better enhanced laws and
regulations regarding whistleblower protection laws
for any state or municipal employee. While there are
some laws and regulations that currently exist, they
are not being enforced by leadership in Frankfort or
by the courts. These whistleblowers are oftentimes
the very people on the front lines of our safety and security here in Kentucky. The fear that exists by these
citizens and taxpayers of simply exposing any type
of waste, fraud, abuse of authority, and corruption is
palpable and justified. No improvements or corrections can be made without first being exposed and
identified. This fear of retaliation by employees in
Kentucky who are simply trying to do their jobs is
flagrant and must be stopped.

- State lawmakers must pass uniform, meaningful laws
and regulations regarding the use of body cameras by
law enforcement personnel.

- Finally, until someone with authority has the courage to uproot the cliques and good ol' boy systems
and make serious changes, then citizens will continue to be harmed and those who inflict the harm will
continue to escape accountability—while no one's
watching.

Sources

- Kentucky Energy and Environmental Cabinet, Custodian of Records
- Kentucky Department of Environmental Protection (DEP), Custodian of Records
- City of Somerset, Custodian of Records
- Pulaski County Sheriff's Department, Custodian of Records
- Somerset Police Department, Custodian of Records
- Somerset Wastewater Treatment Plant (WWTP), Custodian of Records
- Kentucky Office of the Attorney General, Custodian of Records
- Pulaski County Clerk's Office, Custodian of Records
- Trial Transcripts (Commonwealth vs. Sam Baker)
- Supreme Court of Kentucky Opinion and Order (2022-SC-0426-0A); IN RE: Joseph J. S. Flynn, Pulaski Circuit Court Clerk
- Kentucky State Police, Custodian of Records
- Bill Estep, a Great Investigative Reporter for the *Lexington Herald Leader*
- The Mayo Clinic
- The American Psychological Association (APA)

- Andrew Bustamante, Ex-CIA Spy
- *News Break Magazine*
- The Kentucky Center for Investigative Reporting

Case Law Research/References

Kentucky State Police/Commonwealth of Kentucky Appellant v. SGT. Kevin Burton; LT. Frank Chad Taylor; and SGT. Mike Gary Antes Appellees; SGT. Kevin Burton; LT. Frank Chad Taylor; and SGT. Mike Gary Antes Cross-Appellants v. Kentucky State Police/Commonwealth of Kentucky Cross-Appellee; NO. 2022-CA-1028-MR, NO. 2022-CA-1108-MR

Bryant v. Pulaski County Detention Center, 330 S.W.3d 461

United States v. Taylor, 663 F. Supp. 2d 1170, 1180 (D.N.M. 2009)

United States vs. Diaz, No. CR 05-00167 WHA (N.D. Cal. Feb. 12, 2007)

United States v. Monteiro, 407 F. Supp. 2d 351, 372 (D. Mass. 2006)

U.S. v. Glynn, 578 F. Supp 2nd 567, 2008

Daubert v. Merrell Dow Pharm., Inc., 509 U.S. 579, 589-90, 113 S.Ct. 2786, 2794-95, 125 L.Ed.2d 469 (1993)

Mitchell v. Commonwealth, 908 S.W.2d 100, 101-02 (Ky. 1995) (adopting *Daubert* in Kentucky), *overruled in part on other grounds by Fugate v. Commonwealth*, 993 S.W.2d 931, 937 (Ky. 1999).

Daubert, 509 U.S. at 597, 113 S.Ct. at 2798

Elsayed Mukhtar v. Cal. State Univ., 299 F.3d 1053, 1063 (9th Cir. 2002), by requiring a preliminary determination that proffered expert testimony meets the reliability standards of KRE 702. *Mitchell*, 908 S.W.2d at 102.

Fleming v. State, 194 Md. App. 76, 100-01 (2010)

Rochkind v. Stevenson, 471 Md. 1 (2020)

Commonwealth v. Wilson, 2022-CA-1299-MR, 06-30-2023 – Commonwealth of Kentucky Appellant v. Quartez Wilson Appelle.